STORIE DEI

37

FABRIZIO RICCIARDELLI

A Short History of Florence

MAURO PAGLIAI EDITORE

In cover: Giuseppe Zocchi (1717-1767)
The Piazza della Signoria in Florence
Oil on canvas, 57x87 cm - Private collection

1st edition: July 2019
1st reprint: June 2022

www.mauropagliai.it

© 2019 Edizioni Polistampa
Via Livorno, 8/32 - 50142 Firenze
Tel. 055 73787
info@polistampa.com - www.leonardolibri.com

ISBN 978-88-564-0417-3

CONTENTS

PREFACE

Florence is the place where, between the fourteenth and sixteenth centuries, intellectuals, artists and scientists produced a social change so great that it transformed one of the many city-states of communal Italy into a crucial hub for the rebirth of world culture. Florence is the homeland of Dante Alighieri, who was seen by Francesco De Sanctis (1817-1883) as the means for forging Italian identity through the identification of the poet's birthplace with the national language, literature and culture. In the United States, through the vision of the scholar Charles Singleton (1909-1985), Dante became the emblem of the man who does not seek a relationship with God through the pope, a sort of visionary prophet inspired by the Bible who corresponds to the ideals of Puritan America. Florence is the city of Giotto, and thus of the revolution in painting which anticipated the Renaissance, but it is also the city of Filippo Brunelleschi and Leon Battista Alberti, the two greatest creators and theorists of the new architecture founded on a knowledge of classical antiquity.

Florence, too, is the city of Leonardo Bruni, the champion of civic humanism, who stood up to the despotism promulgated by the dukes of Milan. It was also the site of Savonarola's preaching, the precursor, in his thundering denunciation of the vanity of the patrician class and the corruption of the Roman curia, of the Protestantism which Donald Weinstein has read as anticipating middle-class morality. It is the city of Michelangelo's *David*, of Botticelli's *Spring* and *Birth of Venus* and the dome of Florence Cathedral, masterpieces replicated countless times in the media and over time raised to the role of icons of Renaissance art and technology. It is the city of Niccolò Machiavelli, the theorist of the 'ruler' (prince), who supported republicanism and revealed to the people the injustice and violence of political power, showing them by contrast the value of liberty.

Over the years the myth of Florence has continued to exist, becoming consolidated in the second half of the nineteenth century when Florence became capital of the new Kingdom of Italy (1865-71). It is in this period that the myth of the Florentine Republic enters the Anglo-American Academy, and this historical context Florence, paradigm of the Renaissance, began to be perceived as one of the founding moments of Western Civilization, passing from Greece at the time of Pericles to Republican Rome and on to the examples of the city-states in the time of Dante, consolidating and further expanding the crucial value of its history in the vanguard of Western culture as a whole.

ACKNOWLEDGEMENTS

This book presents the history Florence essentially as a cornerstone in the tradition of Western Civilization. Florence is a cultural paradigm through which, even today, new generations can trace the origins of the values of democracy, freedom, rational thought, individualism, scientific method and the capacity for critical reflection that underlie their way of living and their political thought.

I am deeply grateful to the Kent State University environment through which I organize talks, round tables and seminars on the origins of Modern Democracy (and beyond), as well as for promoting a variety of initiatives in the field of political and cultural studies. Todd Diacon, Marcello Fantoni, and I have an ongoing and stimulating dialogue which involves our work as administrators of a huge North American state university such as Kent State University, reminding each other in our intense discussions that, because of its history, Florence is the place where our students became, are becoming, and will become global citizens.

My greatest debt of gratitude is owed to Laura Fenelli, who has carefully read the manuscript with meticulous care and discussed it with me at every stage, offering me numerous valuable suggestions. As always, I am indebted to Humfrey Butters, who continues to read me with great attention, care and competence, and who never gets tired of offering me his valuable advice and suggestions.

My final words, as always, go to my wife Federica and to my daughter Elena, without whom this book could not exist.

Florence, 19 July 2019

THE ROMAN CITY (59 BC - 1138)

Sometime between the tenth and eighth century BC, the Italics, an Indo-European population from the north, settled in the area of what is now Florence where the Arno River was narrow enough to be crossed easily. Subsequently, another group, the Etruscans, decided to abandon the valley: they selected a hill north of the river to build a fortress surrounded by huge walls from which they could control traffic on the plain below. This marked the birth of Fiesole, six kilometers from the Arno, the city that would dominate northern Tuscany from the seventh to the second century BC. During the first century BC, the Roman republic intensified relationships with what is now northern Italy, but was then known as Gallia Cisalpina, or Cisalpine Gaul. For this reason, the point at the foot of the Fiesole hill that crosses the middle course of the Arno became more important. Tradition tells us that in 59 BC, in order to control Arno 'traffic' and make it easier to reach the Po Valley, the Roman general Julius Caesar established a colony on the north bank of the river in the area that had up to then been part of the city of Fiesole. The new colony was located where the small river, the Mugnone, flows into the Arno, which was the easiest point to defend. It was called *Florentia*, and most probably owed its name to the *Floralia* or *Ludi Florales*, the games instituted in the third century BC in honor of Flora, the Italic goddess of spring flowering.

Florence, a small settlement of just fifty blocks, was a typical Roman colony. The urban agglomeration, located entirely in the area north of the river, was a rectangle with two main streets, the *cardo* and the *decumanus* that connected the four gates and intersected at a right angle in the main square, the so-called *forum* with the temple dedicated to the Capitoline Triad, Jupiter, Juno and Minerva, the three most important divinities of the Roman world. The new colony was located where it was relatively easy to cross the Arno; it was also possible to sail down the river to the Tyrrhenian Sea, and this guaranteed the city's future development. At the end of the second century BC, the extension of the Via Cassia, the Roman consular road connecting *Florentia* to Rome, the capital, led to the construction of a bridge that improved traffic and replaced the ferry that had been used to cross the river.

Around the first century AD, some Eastern merchants from Pisa settled in Florence bringing economic growth to the new Roman colony as well as the cult of Isis, the Egyptian goddess of motherhood, fertility and magic. By around the third century AD the population of Florence had grown to ten thousand, and an aqueduct to bring water directly from Monte Morello, located northwest of the city, was built to guarantee a steady supply of water.

A radical change took place in the second century AD when some Syrian merchants brought Christianity to the city. The first saints to be venerated were the deacon Lawrence who had been martyred in Rome in 258, and Saint Felicity, martyred in Carthage early in the third century, during the reign of Septimius Severus (193-211 AD). Her cult developed on the south bank of the Arno close to where the Ponte Vecchio now stands and where the church of Santa Felicita was built in the ninth century. But *Florentia* also had its own martyr. In 250, during the persecutions ordered by the Roman Emperor Decius, Minias, a Roman soldier according to one legend or perhaps an Armenian king passing through the city, was decapitated. To show where he wanted to be buried, he picked up his head and miraculously carried it up a hill south of the city which is now called the San Miniato hill.

It is difficult to determine whether the local Christian community had a bishop at its head prior to the third century. There is certain information only from the fourth century: Bishop Felix is documented in 313 followed by Zenobius, who met Ambrose, the bishop of Milan when he came to the city in 394 to consecrate the first basilica built here after Christianity was legalized. The church was dedicated to the martyr, Saint Lawrence.

Starting in the sixth century, after the fall of the Roman Empire when the city was losing its political importance because of the Germanic invasions, the cult of Reparata, the saint from the Holy Land began to spread. Her feast day is October 8, commemorating the day in 406 when the city was delivered from the hordes of Radagaisus, king of the barbarian Goths. However, Florence was destroyed by Totila, the Ostrogoth king, in 552. The walls that had been built by the Byzantines, the successors of the Eastern Roman Empire, in 541-544 inside the early Roman colony did nothing to protect the city.

During the sixth century, the northern part of the Italian peninsula fell to the Germanic Lombards and Florence, too, became part of their kingdom. When Theodelinda, the Lombard queen, converted to Christianity two important sanctuaries were built in the city: the Baptistery, an octagonal structure dedicated to Saint John the Baptist, and the precursor of the Romanesque baptistery we see today, and the church of San Michele Arcangelo, which later became known as Orsanmichele, and around the eighth century replaced a primitive oratory located on what is now Via de' Calzaiuoli.

Lombard dominion was nevertheless perceived as distant: Florence's central position in the middle of the peninsula exposed the city to the surprise attacks and influence of the Byzantine exarchs still in Ravenna. On the other hand, the Lombards did not seem very interested in Florence. They rarely used the central Bologna-Pistoia-Florence route for their north-south communications: it was too exposed to enemy actions and they preferred the more westerly and apparently safer Cisa Pass. This increased the importance of the Via Francigena – the road that started in France, continued to Milan and Pavia, via Piacenza and arrived at Sarzana, south of the Apennines – making it the main route between northwestern Europe and Rome. As a result of the development of the Via Francigena, the city of Lucca, situated on the road, became the capital of the Lombard duchy in Tuscany. The transformation of Lucca into the capital of the duchy had important consequences for the history of Florence, located on a road that events made secondary, and subordinate to both the capital and to Pisa, which was a crucial outlet to the sea. However, the fact of being secondary and distant from the roads usually traveled by the political leaders, allowed Florence to survive in tranquil independence, laying the foundations of the city's propensity towards political freedom.

A radical change in the political management of the area began after the Carolingians conquered the Lombard kingdom. Each diocese, that is, each territorial subdivision of the Christian community, was assigned a count who, in turn, appointed his vassals. This political reorganization fostered the development of the cities, including Florence. Located on the banks of the Arno, it began to attract the inhabitants of Fiesole who had long been excluded from trade because of their isolated hilltop position. In 854, the Carolingian Emperor Lothar I united the counties of Fiesole and Florence, establishing Florence as the seat of the count. This marked the end of the county of Fiesole and, by absorbing the few parishes of Fiesole, Florence became the center of the biggest county in Tuscany. By this time Florence had grown considerably: the countryside around the city, the so-called *contado*, was nearly twice the size of all the others in the area, extending from the Apennines in the north to the immediate surroundings of Siena in the south, and from the county of Arezzo in the east and to the westerly county of Pistoia.

The Hungarians (Magyars) invaded Tuscany in the tenth century. The population of Florence increased because many peasants sought refuge in the city that was now protected by a new circle of walls, the third built to defend it from invaders. As further proof of the city's growth and the revival of trade, these walls included part of the ancient Roman walls and encompassed the *borghi*, the areas located south of the early Roman colony between the old walls and the river. Economic progress and population growth continued throughout the eleventh century so that the widow of Uberto, Margrave of Tuscany and owner of an entire district inside the walls, ordered the construction of the Badia Fiorentina (between 967 and 969) in memory of her husband and, along with the Baptistery it became one of the most important places of worship in Christian Florence. Then, it was the Margrave Ugo († 1001) who furthered the city's unstoppable development when he decided to move from Lucca and settle in Florence. Lastly, the friendship between the Emperor Henry II and Bishop Hildebrand led to the foundation of the monastery and church, between 1014 and 1050, on the San Miniato hill on the site where the early Florentine martyr had chosen to be buried.

We must remember that when Florence was just beginning to become a real city, Pisa had already achieved greatness and power as a result of its huge trading empire. Florence, however, was an important center for debate about Church reforms. The knight Giovanni Gualberto spoke out vehemently against the corruption within ecclesiastical institutions. The monastery he founded in 1038 at Vallombrosa, on a high, wooded hill overlooking the bend in the Arno, became one of the institutions dedicated to a purer and less corrupt religiosity.

Perhaps it was because of the existence of the monastery that, in 1055, Florence hosted a council presided over by the pope and attended by the Emperor Henry III and one hundred and twenty bishops. Two years later, in 1057, Godfrey of Lorraine, the new Margrave of Tuscany and brother of Pope Stephen IX, chose Florence as his permanent home while the bishop Gérard de Boulogne, who became Pope Nicholas II (1059-1061) decided to maintain the seat of the papacy in Florence and ordered that when the time came he be buried in the city.

Florence's role as one of the main centers of Christianity continued through the dramatic conflict between Pope Gregory VII and the Emperor Henry IV. Florence sided with Matilda of Canossa, Margravine of Tuscany, who was a strong ally of the pope. The fourth circle of walls, following the most extensive paths of the previous ones, now reached as far as the Arno and was completed in 1078. Its sturdiness was proved by the fact that in 1110 it withstood the ten-day siege by Henry IV who was finally forced to withdraw. As a reward for the support she received in the struggle against the emperor, Matilda granted the Florentines many privileges that furthered the city's development. Thanks to these concessions, the most influential citizens, including the *ministeriales* (the agents of the bishop, the viscount and the religious institutions invested with military and political powers) attempted to organize and then eliminate and take over the powers of the viscount (the lay authority) and of the bishop (the religious authority) in controlling the city and the *contado*. In 1068, Pietro Igneo, a monk from Vallombrosa, subjected himself to a trial by fire to prove the strength of his faith: the defeated bishop of Florence was accused of simony, that is selling ecclesiastical offices, and was forced to withdraw in the face of the people's hostility.

Starting in 1113, Florence became the site of conflicts between the emperor's representatives and the noble Alberti family: both wanted to inherit the property of the last of the Carolingian counts and then of Matilda. Imperial power was furthered weakened when Henry V, the last emperor of the Salian dynasty, died in 1125 and many pretenders to the throne made their voices heard. Florence conquered and destroyed Fiesole during the same year, leaving only the cathedral and the bishop's residence standing. The great victory over Fiesole, that was promptly recorded by the main Florentine chroniclers, placed the city at the hub of Tuscan political-economic dynamics. Florence now controlled a huge district where it had no rivals. This power was also displayed in new forms of common rituals: in 1127 the traditional ceremony in which Florentines lit candles in the Baptistery on the feast of Saint John the Baptist was imposed on all the towns and hamlets in the district. Florence exerted her supremacy over all the subordinate cities, as symbolized by the saint who would gradually become the city's main patron, John the Baptist.

Giuseppe Zocchi (1717-1767), *The Piazza della Signoria in Florence*, oil on canvas, 57x87 cm, Private collection.

Map of the first Roman urban colonial establishment of Florence: depicting the surrounding walls,
the *cardo* and the *decumanus*.

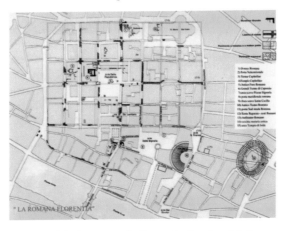

The establishment of *Florentia* in the Adrianea
period, when the city experienced exceptional development, with the indication of the principle
monuments.

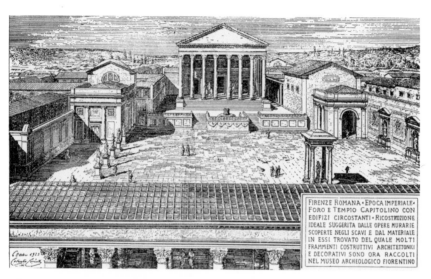

FIRENZE ROMANA · EPOCA IMPERIALE ·
FORO E TEMPIO CAPITOLINO CON
EDIFIZI CIRCOSTANTI · RICOSTRUZIONE
IDEALE SUGGERITA DALLE OPERE MURARIE
SCOPERTE NEGLI SCAVI E DAL MATERIALE
IN ESSI TROVATO DEL QUALE MOLTI
FRAMMENTI COSTRUTTIVI ARCHITETTONICI
E DECORATIVI SONO ORA RACCOLTI
NEL MUSEO ARCHEOLOGICO FIORENTINO

The Forum and Capitol of Roman Florence located in the area now occupied by Piazza della Repubblica. The position of the Capitol, a temple dedicated to Giove, Giunone and Minerva, corresponds to the north-west area of the actual piazza, with the front facing towards the Colonna dell'Abbondanza.

Giorgio Vasari (1511-1574), *The Foundation of Florence* (XVI century), Salone dei Cinquecento, Palazzo Vecchio, Florence.

The Golden Florin (1252-1303).

Bernardi Daddi (1290-1348), *Madonna of Mercy* (1342), Bigallo Museum, Florence.

The devastation of Florence on the part of Totila in a miniature of ms. Chigiano L VIII 296 from the Vatican Library, f. 36r (1.III,1).

Archivio di Stato di Firenze, *Statuti del Comune di Firenze, Ordinamenta Iustitiae* (Ordinances of Justice), 1, f. 1r, Florence, 18 January 1293. The Ordinances of Justice were promoted by Giano della Bella 'ad fortificationem, augumentum et conservationem felicium Ordinamentorum iustitie actenus editorum'.

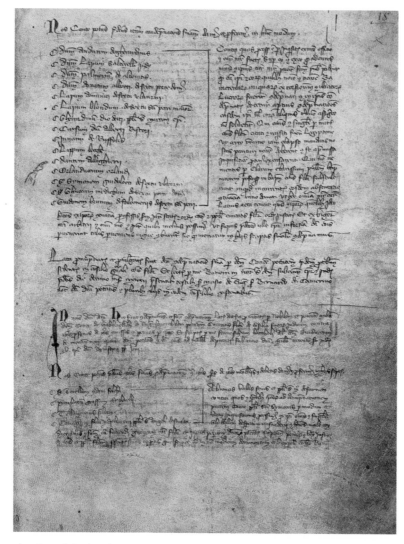

Il Libro del Chiodo, Capitani di Parte, Numeri Rossi, 21, Archivio di Stato, Florence.

Domenico di Michelino, *Our Lady Protecting the Innocents*, Hospital of the Innocents Gallery, Florence.

Domenico di Michelino (1417-1491), *Dante and the Three Kingdoms* (1465), Museo dell'Opera del Duomo, Florence.

Anonymous of the XIX century, *The Arno and Ponte alle Grazie from Ponte Vecchio*, oil on canvas, Pitti Palace Gallery of Modern Art, Florence.

Bicci di Lorenzo (c. 1373-1452), *Consacration of St. Egidio* (1430s), Ospedale di Santa Maria Nuova, Florence.

Benozzo Gozzoli (ca. 1420-1497), *The Procession of the Magi* (around 1459),
Palazzo Medici Riccardi, Florence.

Sandro Botticelli, *Adoration of the Magi*, 1475 ca., the Uffizi Gallery, Florence.

Domenico Ghirlandaio (1449-1494), *Birth of John the Baptist* (1485-90), Tornabuoni Chapel, Santa Maria Novella, Florence.

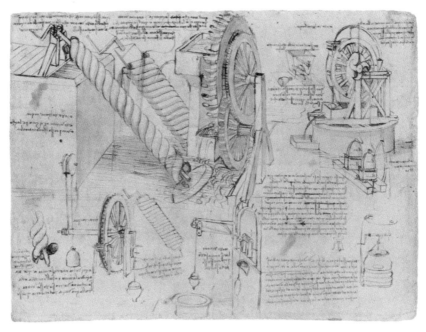

The paper 26r of the *Atlantic Code* (1478-1518), conserved in the Library Ambrosiana of Milan.

2.

THE CITY-STATE (1138-1216)

By conquering Fiesole, Florence proved that it was strong and had enhanced skills in political organization. This autonomous organization of the Florentine community is on record in a document from 1138 that mentions the names Burellus, Florenzitus, Broccardus, Servolus as the city's first consuls. It is possible, however, that the institution of the consulate dated from a few years earlier and that the Florentines had established a Commune, that is an independent governing body, without the emperor's formal consent. When Matilda of Canossa died in 1113, in fact, the inhabitants of Florence took over all the powers that she had not yet granted them and, unlike what was happening in the other city-states throughout northern-central Italy, it did not fight against any bishop to impose its power. The bishop of Florence represented the community with the outside world, but did not exercise power over the city as he could have. In 1154 the imperial legate granted the commune both civil and criminal jurisdiction over the *contado*. This was a *de facto* recognition of Florence as a city-state even though the commune was officially established under the terms of the Treaty of Constance, when the Holy Roman Emperor Frederick Barbarossa, who had been defeated by the Lombard League, was forced to recognize the independence of the Italian communes.

During the second half of the twelfth century, the commune of Florence was led by twelve consuls, two at a time on rotation every two months. Sources tell us that, starting in 1167, alongside the consuls who represented executive power there were two councils of *boni homines* whose duties were to consult and decide: the *Consiglio dei Cento* [Council of the Hundred] and the *Consiglio dei Centocinquanta* [Council of the Five Hundred]. Four Sundays a year, the popular *Assemblea*, or Parliament, met in the cathedral of Santa Reparata for the purpose of ratifying the consuls' actions, approving treaties with

17

other communes or foreign powers, and ratifying briefs and statutes, the documents that defined each official's duties. The first Florentine statute dates from 1159, but unfortunately it does not specify either the requirements for citizenship or for participating in the *Assemblea*.

Official documents, however, do give the names of the first consuls elected in the Commune of Florence indicating that they came from the city's noble families. During the twelfth century, there were lay categories operating alongside Church officials: the bishop, the members of the Cathedral chapter (that is, the body comprising the canons who celebrated religious services in the cathedral), and the congregation of the monasteries, the chaplains, the vicars and the twenty-four parishes of the city's four districts. The local nobility consisted of very different families. Some descended from the old feudal lines and had always lived in Florence like the Uberti and Adimari. Others, such as the Buondelmonti and Ubaldini, were landowners in the *contado* that the Commune had conquered and forced to live in the city, others again were families, such as the Visdomini and Tosinghi, that had acquired noble rank for having served the bishop or viscount. In addition to the noble families, each of which built tower-houses to protect the city from all potential threats, the social alliance consisted of agents of the bishop and viscount, the many illegitimate descendants of clerics who had often illegally acquired their wealth from Church revenues, merchants engaged in foreign trade, artisans and, lastly, the immigrants who had recently abandoned the *contado* in favor of city life.

In the mid-twelfth century the groups that gravitated towards the city were the societies of horse soldiers and of merchants. The former, known as the *cavalleria*, were the soldiers, whether noble or not, who could equip themselves with weapons and horses and serve in the commune's militia at their own expense. They were the backbone of the city's security, an integral part of the army that consisted mostly of citizen foot soldiers and the nobles, the knights, who held positions of power. The rich who were not nobles served the commune; they tried to imitate the lifestyles of knights and nobles and enter the nobility either through knightly investitures or by marrying into titled families. As the name suggests, the merchants' society included all those who in engaged in trade.

These two groups found themselves side-by-side defending the city as mounted fighters and in 'business' since many noble families did not scorn the idea of becoming richer through trade. While in the early phase of the commune the *milites*, the noble mounted warriors, had exclusive control of the consulate, the merchants gradually began rising in status between 1150 and 1180. Their prestige is also evident in the fact that the commune appointed them to maintain and restore important religious buildings such as the Baptistery of San Giovanni and the Basilica of San Miniato al Monte. The *carroccio*, the wagon that carried the commune's banners into battle, was conserved in the Baptistery, and the militia's battle cry was 'San Giovanni!'.

In the twelfth century, power was in the hands of the noble families and those which, though not noble, wished to emulate the nobility. At this time, new sources of wealth for the city and driving forces of the economy were the trade in textiles and money lending. Starting in the twelfth century, Florentine merchants began buying high quality cloth in Flanders and France. They imported excellent dyeing products from the East: *kermes*, cochineal insects and red wood for crimson and carmine red, and indigo for blue. Mixing these organic substances with alum, also obtained from the East and used as a mordant for fixing the colors, allowed the Florentine merchants to dye the beautiful fabrics from northern Europe with the rich dyes from the Levant. The Florentines stretched, sheared and decorated the fabrics to produce the most sumptuous textiles in the West and sell them to the wealthiest customers.

This simple and successful concept was the basis of Florence's economic development for years to come. The global reputation of the Florentine dyeing industry, which acquired the necessary raw materials from port cities such as Pisa, Genoa and sometimes Venice, is borne out by the fact that when, in the sixteenth century, the city of Toulouse in France established its splendor on woad (*Isatis tinctoria*), a flower with a deep blue color, the dyeing power of the substance was measured in the Florentine currency, that is in florins, just like the purity of gold is measured in karats. Florence became one of the most important trading centers in Europe and its merchants invested part of their profits in banking, lending money to private parties and institutions at rates varying from 15 to 25%.

This economic development, in which industry went in tandem with banking, made it necessary to protect the roads from the landowners who still lived in the castles throughout the *contado* and harassed merchants traveling for business by imposing tolls. To defend its interests, the city-state of Florence sent its armies on expeditions against the great nobles of the area such as the Guidi and the Alberti. In spite of this outlay of energy, in 1175 the commune of Florence was able to expand its territories to the possessions of Siena, the most powerful and feared of all nearby rival cities. But Florence did not only wage wars. The city-state was committed to promoting and protecting its main business, that is trade, by establishing fruitful diplomatic relations with all the cities along the roads and the ports where merchant ships called. The government of Florence entered into agreements with Lucca and Pisa, the former because it was the administrative capital of the region and the latter because of its importance as a seaport. Both cities had the imperial privilege of coining silver.

Immigration from the *contado* to the city continued without interruption throughout the twelfth century. The peasants started settling outside the city gates establishing the so-called *borghi* on the streets parallel to and at the base of the walls. In the space of three years, from 1172 to 1175, the population grew by approximately 25,000 and new walls were built encompassing all the *borghi*, bringing the city's area to 136 acres, nearly three times the size of the Roman settlement that had been estimated at around fifty acres. The city's size, and increasing complexity made it necessary to create administrative districts called *sestieri* [wards].

GUELPHS AND GHIBELLINES (1216-1237)

At the end of the twelfth century, Florence found itself, on the one hand, having to maintain and increase its influence in Tuscany to guarantee the free circulation of goods in order to further economic development, while on the other, it had to deal with the changes brought about by a growing population. In terms of foreign policy, the Commune of Florence succeeded in abolishing the toll at Fucecchio, a town in the lower Arno Valley, in mounting a military action against the fortified city of Semifonte, which it conquered and razed to the ground in 1202, and in taking over Poggibonsi in 1208 thereby extending its authority to the borders of the *contado* of Siena. Florence was a city-state and the commune began developing ever more efficient methods for increasing resources and power. In terms of domestic policy, the city had problems related to the election of the consuls who, at that time, were almost all nobles.

The growing numbers of merchants and traders belonged to a social group that did not yet participate in the government. The pressure from these rising groups led to the replacement of the consular system with the regime of the *Podestà*. He served as a magistrate and was initially chosen from among Florentines and later from foreigners; many other communes in Italy had already created the position to ensure domestic peace and tranquility. In 1193 Florence elected Gherardo Caponsacchi, from a local family, as first *Podestà* and granted him executive powers. From the beginning of the thirteenth century, the *Podestà* was a foreigner so that he could, at least in theory, be impartial about matters concerning the city's domestic politics. The *Podestà* had to be a skilled administrator and a military leader, a statesman who could guide the city towards good government and a commander to lead the city's army, in other words he had to combine the skills of a jurist and a soldier. The profession of arms belonged to the nobles and the *Podestà*, who had to be knowledgeable about criminal and civil law, was chosen from amongst the scions of the aristo-cracies of friendly cities.

The establishment of the *Podestà* coincided with the development of Florentine trade on a European scale between the twelfth century and the thirteenth. The first guilds were created in this changing so-ciety. They were lay associations established for the defense and pur-suit of their members' common goals. The associations arose from the need for unity at a time of a major economic opening. The growing number of traders who had been city artisans or who had been members of the rural bourgeoisie and immigrated to Florence illus-trated the need to maintain the domestic market. Following the cre-ation of the Merchants' Guild [*Arte dei Mercanti*] that can be traced back to 1182, other groups began uniting in specialized guilds or *arti* as they were called: skinners and furriers [*Arte dei Vaiai e Pellicciai*], whose members were active and documented in the city from the first half of the twelfth century; the money changers [*Arte dei Cambiatori*], established in 1202; judges and notaries [*Arte dei Giudici e dei Notai*] and wool manufacturers [*Arte della Lana*], both founded in 1212. Each guild drafted its own, legally binding, Statutes, and ruled in disputes among members or among the members and their workers. The silk guild [*Arte della Seta*], that was also known as '*Por Santa Maria*' after the street leading to the Ponte Vecchio where silk fabrics were sold, drew up its statutes in 1308, while the guild of physicians and apothe-caries [*Medici e degli Speziali*] drafted by-laws in 1313.

Via Calimala is the southern section of the ancient Roman *cardo* be-tween what is now Via Por Santa Maria and Piazza della Repubblica, the site of the ancient forum. The street name, Via *Calimala*, that has been twisted over the centuries to the point of becoming an enigma for etymologists, led to the name of the *Arte dei Mercanti* being changed to *Arte di Calimala*. This section of the street was home to workshops that specialized in dyeing and finishing the fabrics that Florentine merchants purchased beyond the Alps at the fairs in Champagne and which, after being processed in the city, were sent to Southern Italy and in Messina were loaded onto ships bound for the East. The Champagne fairs, refer-ring to a series of fairs that, starting from the twelfth century, were held in the county of Champagne in northeastern France: once a year in the cities of Lagny and Bur-sur-Aube, twice a year in Provins and Troyes.

The Calimala workshops in Florence made clothing from the most beautiful fabrics in all of the Christian West, the so-called *pannilana*, or wool cloth. It was a business that attracted so many workers and visitors that in 1218 it became necessary to build the *Ponte Nuovo* or New Bridge – now the Ponte alla Carraia, downstream from what was already being called the Ponte Vecchio. A third bridge was added in 1237, the Ponte Rubaconte, today's Ponte alle Grazie. The city was expanding and this, in turn, led to the birth of the first settlements of the mendicant orders just outside the city walls: the Franciscan convent of Santa Croce, and the Dominican Santa Maria Novella, along with the Ospedale di San Gallo, to assist the poor and pilgrims.

However, the hoped-for pacification of the parties heralded by the creation of the *Podestà* in 1193 was followed by a series of vendettas which, starting in 1216 set two groups of families against one another: two political associations divided into the Guelph and Ghibelline factions. According to one almost legendary version, which must contain elements of truth, it was a dispute during a wedding feast between a Buondelmonti and a Fifanti that triggered the quarrel between the two families. A young Buondelmonti, who had broken his promise to marry a girl of the Amidei family, was killed by the relatives and associates of the dishonored bride and from then on feuds and vendettas continued without cease. The Guelphs gathered around the Buondelmonti, the Donati and many other families, while the Ghibellines supported the Fifanti, Amidei, Uberti, Lamberti and the counts of Gangalandi who, together with the girl's parents, had instigated the tragedy. During those same years, Italy's loyalties were split between two candidates for the succession of the Holy Roman Empire, Otto IV of Brunswick on one side and the young Frederick II, son of Henry VI, on the other. Since Henry had supported the Fifanti and Uberti in 1193, these families now, along with many allies, sided with Frederick, while the Buondelmonti, Adimari and their friends and relatives supported Otto. The former, therefore, were champions of the Ghibelline faction, from the name of one of the Hohenstaufen castles, Weiblingen, which Frederick Barbarossa proudly added to his title; the latter favored the Guelph cause because Otto belonged to the Welfs family. In actual fact, the struggle over the imperial election was a distant matter and the opposition between the two groups of families was due to personal animosities and business competition. Their private dispute became part of the greatest public conflict of the Middle Ages that set the pope and the emperor against each other as they vied for political supremacy in the Christian West.

4.

THE RISE OF THE *POPOLO* (1237-1293)

In 1237, after Emperor Frederick II's victory at Cortenuova over the cities of the Lombard League allied with the pope, the Ghibellines in Florence suggested a policy of rapprochement with the emperor. For this reason, the new *Podestà* was a member of the emperor's family and from that moment on, the Ghibelline-faction families took over power in the city. In order to win the favor of the middle class, the Ghibellines authorized the guilds to establish the *Popolo*, an autonomous organization headed by two captains who shared power alongside the *Podestà*. This was an unexpected broadening of the government's social base and from that time on governing was no longer the sole prerogative of the nobles.

Early in 1249, Frederick II sent his illegitimate son, Frederick of Antioch, to Florence at the head of a German cavalry expedition which forced the Guelphs to leave Florence and take refuge at Caprona, Montevarchi and other fortified villages in the *contado*. From these strongholds, the Guelphs forced the Ghibellines into a costly war of attrition that was paid for by unpopular increases in taxes. The *Popolo* reacted to the excessive taxation in 1250, and finally removed the Ghibelline nobles from the government of the commune. The sudden death of Frederick II in December of that year led to a quick decline of the Ghibelline forces throughout the peninsula. The exiled Guelphs returned to Florence at the beginning of 1251 and in July, the Ghibellines were banished by the new regime known as *Primo popolo*. This was not an exclusively Guelph government but rather a coalition that attempted to remain equidistant from both factions, so much so that the Ghibellines were soon allowed back to Florence and efforts were made to promote the peace and domestic tranquility that were the essential conditions for expanding the city's economy. For this reason, limits were placed on the heights of all the family towers: throughout the city the towers, symbols of the families' power, were lowered in the quest for an ideal equality among the different factions. The international situation aided the *Popolo's* political actions and the commune's autonomy was considerably strengthened as a consequence of the empire's absence from the scene. This marked the beginning of the period that the Guelph chronicler, Giovanni Villani (1276-1348), described as a happy time in the city's history and one that would be difficult to repeat.

Even though they traditionally championed the papacy and hence the Guelphs, the *Popolo* essentially maintained neutrality vis à vis both the Guelph and Ghibelline factions in order to pursue its political goals. The government of the *Primo Popolo* embodied the strengths of the city's economy which needed positive conditions at home in order to grow. While Florence tried to maintain domestic peace, it pursued an aggressive and expansionistic foreign policy aimed at conquering and controlling the main roads. The development that best explains the needs of the Florentine merchants was the minting of the gold florin in 1252. For many years the coin had the image of Saint John the Baptist on one side and the Florentine lily on the other; it was worth twenty silver florins that is twenty-three karats, and therefore 3.55 grams. It became the new currency unit of the Christian West, but was also used by merchants trading with the Far East. By being the first to mint a gold coin, Florence established itself as a sovereign power and the financial capital of all Christendom.

Even though it did not identify completely with the Guelph faction, the *Popolo* in Florence gradually became increasingly Guelph. In 1258, Manfred – son of Frederick II – who was already King of Sicily and at war with the papacy, took the political initiative in Tuscany and strengthened the Ghibelline faction. The government of Florence was hostile and the Ghibellines, who had to go into exile again, organized their revenge from Siena. Two years later, on 4 September 1260, the Ghibelline troops led by Siena defeated the Guelph army headed by Florence in the bloody battle of Montaperti, near Siena. The government of the *Primo Popolo* collapsed and the Guelph nobles headed for exile – to Lucca or Bologna beyond the Apennines. Nine days later, the Ghibelline exiles who had returned to Florence set up a new government that would quickly deteriorate in a series of unfortunate military operations against the remaining Guelphs. Two new French popes, Urban IV and Clement IV, reorganized the anti-Swabian Guelphs. Charles of Anjou, brother of King Louis IX of France descended to Italy and defeated and killed Manfred on 26 February 1266. The Ghibelline government wavered and in 1267 a French contingent of light cavalry entered the city on Easter night and forced thousands of Ghibellines to leave Florence. The copies of sentences contained in the *Libro del Chiodo* confirm that a huge number of exiles remained outside the city for a long time. Florence was dominated by the magnates who were united in the Guelph party, an authentic governing body that confiscated and managed the Ghibellines' property. Exile had become a political punishment, inflicted on one party when the other gained power, forcing the 'losers' to leave. The exiles allied themselves with the political forces of nearby cities, impacting both the domestic and foreign policies of Tuscany's cities.

The situation in Florence remained static until 1282 when the *Popolo* returned to power and tried to marginalize both the Guelph and Ghibelline magnates, the rich citizens whose ambitions were perceived as threats by the people, not only because of their luxurious lifestyles, but mainly because they fomented discord among the factions in order to gain political advantages. In general, the word 'magnate' referred to the rich and powerful families that belonged to the local oligarchy and could boast ancient feudal origins and a deeply-rooted military tradition.

The city drew up a new constitution based on the government of the *Arti,* the Guelph-dominated merchant and craft guilds; it was a government that aimed at removing the Ghibellines from the city's political life and making them into stateless exiles. Historians have called this regime, headed by the guilds, the *Secondo Popolo.* The Lesser Guilds [*Arti Minori*] were established during the second half of the thirteenth century, and each one had its own statutes. The guild of Wine Sellers [*Arte dei Vinattieri*] was founded in 1266, the Shoemakers [*Calzolai*] already existed in 1273 and the curriers and tanners [*Cuoiai*] is on record as of 1282. However, it was the Greater (or Major) Guilds [*Arti Maggiori*] – Judges and Notaries, Cloth Merchants or Calimala, Moneychangers, Wool Manufacturers and Merchants, Silk Weavers and Merchants or Por Santa Maria, Physicians and Apothecaries, and Furriers and Skinners – that chose the city's governors, the six priors who were elected every two months and held executive powers. Between 1289 and 1290, real power was in the hands of the Greater Guilds, which proceeded to reform the tax system to eliminate the magnates' privileges and abuses.

On 15 December 1292, Giano della Bella (second half of the thirteenth century – 1306) from one of the city's oldest Ghibelline families was elected prior. He quickly grasped the fact that the largest groups could not be excluded from the government much longer: in 1293 he implemented measures that guaranteed the peaceful triumph of the *Popolo* and the elimination of the magnates from Florence. These exceptional measures, known as the *Ordinamenti di giustizia* (Ordinances of Justice), removed the magnates from power and, without sending them into exile, reduced them to the position of citizens without political rights. However, the *Ordinamenti di giustizia* did not bring political equality or democracy which was a concept totally unknown to the people of northern-central Italian city-states in the late Middle Ages. The magnates could no longer be elected to the posts of prior or gonfalonier of justice, that is the head of the priors, or as the chief members of the councils: the *Popolo* drew up a special criminal code ordering violent police actions against the magnates aimed at putting their existence to an end. The campaign to discredit the magnates championed by the government of the *Popolo* centered on the metaphor of the wolf and the lamb. The enclosure of reason, that is the sacred, inviolable city, was defended by the beastly wolves, animals that were as ferocious and rapacious as the magnates. This marginalization, or political cleansing was carried out by using precise and established legislation that was justified by defining the magnates as dangerous men who were harmful to the city's society.

After some amendments, allowing a certain number of magnates to return to the city as *popolani* – common people – and to once again enjoy political rights and normal positions in the city, the city's new social structure became established in the final years of the thirteenth century. By excluding the nobles from public office, power was conferred upon the Greater Guilds [*Arti Maggiori*] and the category of wealthy citizens known as the *popolo grasso*, corresponding more or less to the upper middle class. The new leading families included the Peruzzi, Acciaiuoli, Altoviti, Alberti, Cerretani, Albizi, Strozzi, Pitti and, finally, the Medici, who would reach the heights of power and prestige in the next century.

The City of Arnolfo, Dante and Giotto (1282-1348)

On 11 July 1289, the Guelph army of Florence defeated the Ghibelline forces of Arezzo at Campaldino. The Guelph victory led to increasing Florentine hegemony over Tuscany. It also led to the immediate split of the Guelph party into Black and White factions, stemming from conflicts between the old, blue-blooded aristocrats and the new, moneyed aristocrats. The Donati, an ancient noble family possibly of feudal origins, which had moved to the city in view of the growing financial/economic opportunities offered by the Commune, bore a grudge against the Cerchi, a perfect example of the *gente nuova* – new people, or nouveaux riches – from the *contado* whom the Florentine poet Dante Alighieri (1265-1321) accused of having quickly achieved social status through 'sudden gains' (*Divine Comedy, Inferno*, XVI, v. 73). The old Florentine nobility, represented by the Donati, were indignant about the new status that the Cerchi had acquired not through family lineage but through trade.

The struggle between the Whites and the Blacks was ignited on 1 May 1300 during the celebrations for the arrival of the Spring, attended by many armed young men from both factions who watched the ladies dancing. One of the Blacks wounded Ricoverino dei Cerchi in a brawl in Piazza Santa Trinita. This episode marked the beginning of unbridled discord: in 1301 the Whites were defeated, partly as a result of the intervention of foreign forces led by Charles de Valois, brother of the French king, and were forced into exile; one of them was Dante himself, who never returned to Florence.

Notwithstanding these divisions, Florence reached its financial and demographic peak between the end of the thirteenth century and the beginning of the next. With a population of about 90,000, the city created an extraordinary impression on the contemporary world, like Venice, Milan, and Paris. In the same period, Bologna, with around 50,000 inhabitants, was one of the most populous Italian cities, while the populations of Pisa, Siena and Lucca did not exceed 40,000-50,000. In other urbanized areas of Europe (such as the Netherlands which, in terms of population density were comparable to Tuscany), the most populous city was probably Ghent, which, like Bologna, had approximately 50,000 inhabitants. In Germany, Lübeck, one of the most important cities in the Hanseatic League, had no more than 15,000 inhabitants around 1300, while the population of London, one of the biggest cities in England, probably did not exceed 40,000. Florence was also a city-state with revenues comparable to those of the kingdoms of Naples, Sicily, and Aragon; it was a city with an educational system that guaranteed widespread literacy (at least for males) and commerce able to sustain enough wool production to provide work for one third of the population.

Starting in the second half of the thirteenth century, the commune of Florence enacted a series of what we would call public relations strategies to obtain the political agreement of the upper classes. The city was remodeled to become the image of a shared symbology and proof of a complex history of political and social changes that had taken place over the years. The *civitas* selected areas to share, places where the community symbolically expressed its political, religious and economic identity. The city's domination of the citizenry changed the sacred sites and the symbols of urban memory: the appearance of the city began to change and all the principal civic sites were re-conceived. Interest in urban areas became stronger, more specific and more ambitious. Erecting new buildings became essential and the renewal of the city's layout responded to the political program aimed at strengthening the form of government which promoted it. Architecture became the tool which, more than any other, contributed to the creation of political and social harmony: the city's greatness was measured by the construction or expansion of its architectural symbols, designed to be bigger and grander than ever. The new buildings enhanced the city and contributed to the creation of a shared identity. Political harmony, the essential condition for any concept of a 'state' as a body that could transform the many into one, was pursued by financing imposing public works.

Florence became the theater in which the established order succeeded in masking social tensions and spreading an image of greater political harmony than actually existed. A new circle of walls was erected between 1284 and 1333 enclosing the city within an area of approximately 1,550 acres. Up until 1865, when the walls were demolished to make room for expansion, they continued to encircle the marvels with which the merchants who held power had decided to adorn the city. These included the Baptistery, the sanctuary of the city's patron, Saint John the Baptist: the polychrome marble cladding on the outside corner pillars was completed in a perfect imitation of the old Romanesque intarsias on the sides, and above all, the inside of the octagonal dome was decorated with sparkling mosaics. On 24 June of each year, for the feast of Saint John, the piazza named for the city's patron saint was covered with a twelve meter high canvas awning supported by ropes that were fastened to the facades of the surrounding churches and buildings with iron hooks to shade the participants from the sun and to give the square the appearance of a single protected space. There was dancing in the adjacent streets and the *palio*, a horse race, was run starting from the bridge over the Mugnone outside Porta al Prato, called *'alle Mosse'* [the start], and following a route through Borgo Ognissanti, Via della Vigna Nuova, the Mercato Vecchio, Via del Corso, Borgo degli Albizi, and San Pier Maggiore.

During the same period, construction work began on monuments that were essential for a large and wealthy city that proclaimed its freedom and began using the *Marzocco* [lion], an ancient symbol of power and sovereignty, as one of its emblems. And so, the commune decided to rebuild the cathedral, enlarging it to designs by the architect Arnolfo di Cambio (c. 1240-c. 1302). Since the Eastern Saint Reparata had little prestige and had already been replaced by Saint John the Baptist as the city's patron; the new cathedral, too, was renamed and dedicated to the Virgin of Florence - Santa Maria del Fiore.

In the late Middle Ages, at least in the Western world, it was impossible to create a civic conscience without the spiritual component, in which the forms of communication were always inextricably linked with the symbolism of the relics of the patron saint. Consequently, religious architecture was one of the main tools that, more than others, contributed to the creation of political and social harmony. The city's greatness was measured by the construction or enlargement of the cathedral, which was often claimed to be the largest in Christendom. The cathedral was the religious building that had to embody the political ideals of the government that had sponsored it for the good and peace of the city and its surroundings. The construction or enlargement of the cathedral was one of the main political moves made by each local community to reinforce and embed the concept that the 'state', the sponsor of magnificent architecture, was the true and only guarantor of political stability. The construction of the cathedral was bound to the veneration of the patron saint who, in the main cities of central-northern Italy, was the fulcrum of the cities' collective identity. Then there were the lavish processions, occasions that defined a specific civic ritual which was sometimes characterized by special symbolic gestures and deeds – such as offering candles and banners and releasing prisoners.

Writing about Santa Maria del Fiore, Giovanni Villani stated that the construction of the sacred site was the principal source of civic pride. The commune of Florence commissioned the architect Arnolfo di Cambio to build the cathedral in 1296, a time that, according to the chronicler, coincided with the period of greatest political stability achieved by the government of the *popolo* after the implementation of the *Ordinamenti di giustizia* against the magnates. Arnolfo envisioned a grand cathedral, built to a plan that ideally recalled the shape of a lily, and set a little further back from the Baptistery to leave more space in the square. After Arnolfo died in 1310, work on the cathedral slowed until 1331 when the Arte della Lana, the guild of Wool Merchants, took over patronage of the construction, appointing Giotto to oversee the work (1334). When in 1349 Francesco Talenti (*c.* 1305 - after 1396) took over as director of works, he decided to challenge the other great Tuscan cathedrals, such as that of Pisa, by further enlarging the plan.

The spread of Christianity had made aid and charity basic religious duties. In Florence, in the sacred area of the city, was founded in 1244 the Confraternita di Santa Maria della Misericordia. It was a brotherhood established to provide help to all the needy, and to support invalids, the sick and the poor families, whose status was documented by vouchers that gave them the right to ongoing assistance. Not long afterwards – in 1288 – and once again in the vicinity of the sacred site, Folco Portinari, the father of Dante's beloved Beatrice, founded Santa Maria Nuova, the city's first hospital. It was Monna Tessa, the family's maid and governess to Beatrice, who convinced him to undertake the project; indeed, the stone marking her grave is still visible in the former *Chiostro delle Ossa* at the hospital. Building a hospital was a mission of charity because for a good Christian medical care was necessarily linked to spiritual care. Once again, it is Giovanni Villani who tells us that at the beginning of the fourteenth century Florence had one thousand hospital beds for the needy, a number equal to 1% of the population.

Excavations for the foundations of a bell tower were begun in 1296, again in the same sacred area. The bell tower of Santa Maria del Fiore, decorated with statues of prophets, fine marbles and relief carvings that were intended to illustrate a truly human concept of work, was sponsored by the Florentine government of the *popolo*. With the help of his workshop assistants, the sculptor Andrea Pisano, who had already made the first bronze doors of the Baptistery, created the Planets, the Liberal, Mechanical and Figural Arts, the Virtues and the Sacraments. In sequence, the panels represent the skills of the Florentine master craftsmen, portraying the entire community's security and productivity at the base of the tower that stands in the exact center of the city's sacred area. The composition had to illustrate human activities which, according to scholastic philosophy, were divided into the three categories of *Necessitas*, *Virtus* and *Sapientia*. The relief carvings formed a simple and perfectly legible lexicon for the citizens, a lexicon which – through an elementary series of citations – could be varied, adapted and, above all, understood by everyone. Between 1437 and 1439, Luca della Robbia completed the iconographic program of the bell tower by carving some of the panels for the base on the north side.

In 1294, the government of the *popolo* commissioned Arnolfo di Cambio to build an imposing palace to be the residence of the priors. The new Palazzo della Signoria was much larger than the old Palazzo del Bargello, where the *Capitano del Popolo* and the consuls had lived since 1250, indicating that the new Commune had triumphed over the old consular regime. The *palazzo dei priori*, as it was also called, stands on the site of what had been the ancient Roman theater, near a large piazza, built over the ruins of the Ghibelline Uberti family's homes, and also encompassed the foundations of the old Foraboschi family tower. As a result of these existing buildings and spaces, the palazzo is irregular in shape. This is where the priors lived for the two months they held office. They were protected from attack while – by the same token – enclosing them in a building that resembled a fortress meant that the city could control their actions.

The construction of other large churches, the Franciscan Santa Croce and the Dominican Santa Maria Novella, added two more monuments that were fundamental in the political and social dynamics of the new class in power, the *popolo*. It was only later, during the fourteenth century, that Orsanmichele, a building which had represented the corporative basis of the city's new institutions, was transformed from a grain market into the church of the guilds (1377), and statues of the patron saints of the fourteen guilds were placed in the niches on all four sides early in the fifteenth century.

A CITY OF MERCHANTS (1282-1348)

The merchant class that took power in August 1282 gained strength from the inexorable economic and demographic growth of the century's early decades. Florentine merchants purchased wool in England, cloth in Flanders, and dye substances and alum, an essential mineral for fixing colors, in northern France and the East. Thanks to this huge network they processed, dyed and decorated textiles to sell as finished goods throughout the known world. When Charles of Anjou became king of Sicily with the help of the Florentine Guelph cavalry, the resulting alliance with the Kingdom of Sicily allowed the Florentines to import at attractive prices the grain and cereals essential for feeding a continuously growing urban population. They engaged in this trade in an across-the-board manner – wholesale, retail and semi-wholesale, and they loaned money to the poor, to the clergy, to nobles, kings, emperors and even popes.

But how did a Florentine bank operate? The Calimala merchants opened current accounts for their depositors and debtors and upon receiving orders made payments or collected money from all over the known world. When the Florentines invented the bill of exchange at the end of the thirteenth century, they could even guarantee their clients international exchange of the florin and hence banking-treasury services on a large scale. It worked like this: a merchant would deposit a sum of money in Florence, he could 'travel light' without cash, and with the bill of exchange collect the amount abroad – converted into the local currency – by simply going to a branch office of the Florentine bank. Members of the other Major Guilds breached the boundaries of their respective fields and engaged in this type of business, albeit to a lesser extent than the Calimala merchants. In this way they continued to devote themselves to the manufacture and sale of their goods, while not looking askance at reinvesting part of their capital in lending operations, and sometimes even usury (lending at very high interest rates), a sin that the Church condemned very harshly.

Obviously, when practiced on a large scale such loans entailed considerable risks. The Bardi and Peruzzi families' companies loaned money to the English Crown for a long time. After the beginning of the Hundred Years' War between England and France in 1337, the English king Edward III was no longer able to repay the loans granted by Italian bankers who had given him credit up to the enormous sum of one and a half million florins (900,000 from the Bardi and 600,000 from the Peruzzi). The financial collapse of the two companies began in 1340, culminating in the Peruzzi's bankruptcy in 1343 and that of the Bardi in 1346. The default was caused by the insolvency of the English Crown and by the lack of liquidity typical of the banks in this period, since they tended to invest capital in property making it difficult to pay out the deposited amounts on demand in the event of emergencies. The Bardi and Peruzzi were unable to cover the run on their banks by depositors who, prompted by the 'suspicious climate' and fueled by the gradual worsening of the crisis, rushed to withdraw their money.

The Florentine economy was based on three main activities, trade, industry and banking. In spite of the fact that the city had no direct outlet to the sea, it still managed to become one of the most important markets in Italy and in Europe. The first half of the fourteenth century was the period of greatest splendor for the Wool Manufacturers Guild: it employed about three hundred men who produced approximately one hundred thousand bolts of cloth each year. Alongside the larger businesses, there were others that were more strictly local. The lower classes established the 'Intermediate Guilds' [*Arti Mediane*], the associations of the *rigattieri* (literally 'rag-dealers' that is retail cloth vendors), *telaioli* (weavers); *calzettai* (hosiers), *magliai*, (knitters) *muratori* (builders and stonemasons); *carpentieri* (carpenters), *fabbri ferrai* (blacksmiths locksmiths), occupations that were essential to a continuously growing population. Then there were the *beccai* (butchers) the only middle-class food-related occupation because of the prestige and high cost of meat consumption.

The lower classes made their living from simple, but necessary, occupations: *vinatieri* (vintners-wine dealers); *osti* (innkeepers who provided lodging and food); *oliandoli* (olive oil merchants and provision dealers); *mercanti di sale e di formaggio* (salt and cheese vendors);

conciatori (tanners); *fabbricanti di corazze e di spade* (armorers and swordsmiths); *calderai* (coppersmiths), *cuoiai* (leather workers); *mercanti di legname all'ingrosso* (wholesale lumber merchants); *fornai* (bakers).

The majority of the urban proletariat was made up of cloth workers, the *ciompi*. While the very rich members of the Cloth Merchants Guild would be comparable to the big entrepreneurs of today, the *ciompi* did all the work: weaving, dyeing, scouring, carding; combing and shearing. However, since only the heads of the workshops, and not always all of them, could pay the dues for being active members of the guild, they were 'passive' members, nothing more than salaried employees, paid by the day or week who could not speak in the council or vote in the members' meetings. The merchant class, the *popolo grasso*, ran the government because the priors were chosen exclusively from the Major Guilds, which were also the 'source' of the men who sat on the councils and the *Tribunale della Mercanzia*, the court comprising six foreign lawyers and six local councilors who judged disputes among Florentine merchants. Most of the trade employees and industrial workers were not represented in the management of the guilds nor, therefore, in the city government. This, as we shall see, was one of the great shortcomings of the government of the *popolo* in Florence.

While the urban proletariat was excluded from holding public office, the most affluent men and nobles of the past did not fare much better. As we have seen, according to the *Ordinamenti di giustizia* of 1293, the magnates could not participate in power unless they joined a trade organization. In this way the political and economic power of the Major Guilds transformed the *popolo grasso* into a sort of intellectual elite, and the city's life, development, and prosperity depended on their profitable, fruitful activities. The Florentine companies that conducted business in a huge international arena demanded that all the partners and agents who worked with and for them should develop culturally as well. Consequently, the Major Guilds implicitly also wanted their members to be educated. The theoretical part of such education consisted of reading, writing, arithmetic and learning French, the international language during the thirteenth and fourteenth centuries. Heeding the requests of such businessmen, the commune established schools where the children of the rich Florentine merchant families learned the basics of this modern culture. When the students reached the age of fifteen, they continued their training by working in the family company's banks and branches.

Being successful in business called for a certain mentality, comprising a complete familiarity with all the products of international trade, the routes and transit times, commercial procedures and banking, which was in constant evolution. Such businessmen also needed complete and accurate information, which was constantly updated through continuous correspondence regarding commodity markets throughout the known world and, in general, about political, military and religious events that could impact business. Deciding upon the right transaction required extensive knowledge of affairs: one had to start with definite data and consider not only the profit-making angle, but also how to avoid ruin. A critical spirit and decision-making skills were essential!

THE BLACK PLAGUE (1348)

Between the end of the thirteenth century and the beginning of the fourteenth, what had appeared to be the relentless economic growth of Europe since the year one thousand came to a halt, and the virtuous circle of population growth, agricultural development and increased trade could not sustain the Florentine trading companies' profitability. Farming, in particular, was no longer able to produce enough to feed the growing population and famines became more and more frequent. The most severe famine in Europe lasted from 1315 to 1317, with disastrous effects: many people died because of lack of food and those who did survive were so weakened that they could not fight off disease. The countryside was less protected than the cities, where the authorities made every effort to offset the food shortages through provisioning policies. In his 1798 book, *An Essay on the Principle of Population*, the English economist Thomas Malthus (1766-1834) maintained that population growth needs adequate technological support to overcome natural adversities, since population always grows geometrically (2, 4, 8, 16, 32, 64 etc.) while the means of sustenance increase arithmetically (2, 4, 6, 8, 10, 12 etc.). Malthus explained that, over the course of history the production of resources does not support population growth and therefore, when famine leads to insufficient production of resources and the population continues to grow, more people die from malnutrition.

The plague struck this exhausted and vulnerable population in 1348. The bacillus responsible for the epidemic came from Turkestan; the disease, which had mysteriously disappeared from the West in the eighth century, began showing its effects in 1347 at Caffa, a Genoese colony on the Black Sea. Then the Genoese ships carried it first to Messina, then to Genoa and within a few months to Italy, Spain, France and the rest of Europe, sparing only a very few regions. There are two types of plague: bubonic that is transmitted by flea bites (the fleas first infest rats and then humans) and pneumonic that is spread directly from person to person via breathing and coughing.

The plague struck mainly the poorer classes who were often under-nourished and lived in very unsanitary conditions – easy terrain for the disease to thrive. Within three years roughly 30 million people died of the plague. More than one third of Europe's population was struck down in the countryside and in cities, where dead bodies abandoned by relatives remained unburied in the streets, terrorizing the living and spreading contamination. Fields were not cultivated, workshops were forced to close, convents and monasteries were deserted, the deaths of entire families left houses and palaces empty. Political life was paralyzed. Then, just as it had appeared, at the end of 1350 the Black Death abruptly disappeared from central-western Europe. In actual fact, although the epidemic emergency was over, the plague would continue endemically for a long time, returning every nine to twelve years and halting demographic recovery.

In the Introduction to the 'First Day' of the *Decameron*, the four-teenth-century author Giovanni Boccaccio (1313-1375) speaks of the plague as a black pall of horror that came from the East, proceeding inexorably to Italy and Florence like the advance of a Triumph of Death from which there was no escape. The symptoms of the disease, described by Boccaccio with the concise clarity of a medical report, conveyed the sense of its deadliness and its mystery, a mystery caused by the malevolent influence of the stars or a punishment sent from God. It was a mystery of which one could describe only the phenomenology and the invisible manner it manifested itself, which, would leave its mark on lives for many years to come. The plague was an unknown, it could not be cured, avoided or prevented: only its terrible effects could be ascertained. Boccaccio's description of two hogs that rubbed their snouts in the rags of a poor man who had just died of the plague and began to shake and turn and within a short time died on the spot, remained engraved in the peoples' minds and inevitably impacted social relations.

However, the real plague was the breakdown of all bonds of friendship and family relations, of affections and citizenship. It was the annulment of the common law, the rules established by families and the controls exercised by religious respect. The plague of 1348 forced everyone to desperately seek safety from the disease on his own account, so that the *civitas*, with its rituals, order and rules, was dissolved, lost, annulled. The plague became the metaphor for the dissolution of the republic, governed in a totally partial manner by the guilds, or rather the Major Guilds, the ones that had contributed to the construction of the commune.

The disease had devastating effects from social and economic standpoints. The drop in the prices of farm products and lordly revenues resulting from the decrease in the population diminished the landowners' incomes, while the rise in wages and the consequent improvement of working conditions did not last for long because the owners and the governments almost immediately adopted containment measures. Although it is difficult to establish precise causal relationships, many revolts during the course of the fourteenth century occurred in this troubled climate.

Recurring food shortages, like unemployment, were powerful causes of social unrest and unhappiness during the fourteenth century. Due to the famines, a large percentage of the population was destined to die of starvation, desperation and malaise which, in turn, triggered episodes of collective violence that, albeit in different ways, could always be traced to the need to improve personal or group conditions. In Italy too, hunger and fear created a strong incentive to restore more humane living conditions and caused changes in the power relations among social classes and, in most cases, redefined balances and political models. The scarcity and high prices of food after the famines became the spark that ignited revolts. The famines triggered popular uprisings in Bologna (1311), in Florence (1329, 1335, 1345 and 1347), in Naples (1329), and then in Barletta (1340), in Siena (1303, 1329 and) 1347, in Rome (1329 and 1347) and in Gaeta (1353).

Tensions were heightened by social class differences: the *popolo* was divided into *grasso* and *minuto,* that is those who amassed riches and those who, remaining at the margins, contributed to the wealth of the others with their labor. The objective of the popular uprising that broke out in Florence in 1343, led by a dyer named Bartolomeo del Corazza, was to change the rebels' social conditions, even at the cost of using violence. This rebellion clearly reveals the two opposing identities of the guilds, and the desire of the wage-earners who were excluded from the guilds to join together in associations in order to improve their living conditions.

Another Florentine revolt, this time in 1345, can help us to better understand how the conflict between the *popolo grasso* and the *popolo minuto* spurred courage, and how that friction developed in the wool industry at a time when the Wool Manufacturers Guild was pushing to lower the workers' wages more than usual. The revolt came to head during the government of Walter VI, Count of Brienne, a French nobleman appointed to rule Florence as *signore* between 1342 and 1343. Concerned about the economic crisis and desperate about the unceasing struggles among the factions, the governors of Florence had decided some years earlier to entrust the city to a foreign *podestà* who had no ties to any of the factions. Although Walter's appointment originally had a fixed term, the lower classes, impressed by his early political actions, wanted him to be *podestà* for life. In the years that he controlled Florence, Walter granted the dyers [*Tintori*] and the doublet-makers [*Farsettai*] the right to join together in guilds with the possibility of choosing their own priors, but always under the strict control of his officers. When the dyers' guild was suppressed in 1344 and the salaried workers in the wool industry were forbidden to establish autonomous associations, discontent spread through the city and in the autumn of that year the uprising was quelled and the instigators punished, leaving the rebels deeply dissatisfied.

Ciuto Brandini came onto the scene just a few months later, in May 1345. He was a Florentine carder from the parish of San Pier Maggiore and tried to organize a strike with the aim of establishing a trade association for his fellow workers. The carders worked in wool manufacturing, and their job was to separate the locks and clumps of fiber and align them into threads of varying lengths, a very important process in wool-cloth manufacturing because it allowed the raw material to become a semi-finished product. On the initiative of Ciuto Brandini meetings were held in the city streets, in Piazza Santa Croce and beneath the Loggia dei Servi di Maria, in piazza SS. Annunziata, and the *in pectore* members of those guilds were asked to pay a registration fee. However, the uprising did not succeed and Ciuto and his two sons were arrested on 24 May 1345; they were judged by the *Podestà* and sentenced to death by hanging within a few days. The severity of the punishment – hanging – was due to Brandini's humble social status: accused of having tried to subvert the established order, he was guilty of an immense crime. The period chronicles unanimously condemned Brandini's initiative because it could potentially overthrow the merchant regime, and showed that hanging was not meant only to repress dissent, but also to discredit a worker – *popolano* – who opposed the government, the *popolo*. In the Middle Ages, death by hanging was a punishment for the lower classes. In Brandini's case it clearly showed the disdain the great merchants had for those who dared to destabilize the equilibrium guaranteed by the guilds, and especially those who, through their behavior, could endanger the clearly precarious relationship between the entrepreneurs and the wage-earners.

The reasons for the revolts can be traced to the inability of the governments that rose to power in most central-northern Italian cities during the second half of the thirteenth century to create harmony between management and labor in managing the guild system and the common weal. The case of Florence is paradigmatic if we think of the citizenship papers given to foreigners. The documents dealing with the benefits of Florentine citizenship conserved in the *Provvisioni* in the *Archivio di Stato* in Florence, reveal how difficult it was for foreigners (including Tuscan peasants, according to the organization of the city-state) to become citizens of the Florentine Republic before the plague of 1348, whereas in the decades following the outbreak of the disease the number increased exponentially. From 1288 to 1352 only one foreigner was granted citizenship: on 14 October 1288, Bonaccorso Falchi and his two sons benefitted from that opportunity. After the plague, the drop in population (Florence lost four fifths of its inhabitants) led to slightly broader policies of inclusion for foreigners.

The discrepancy between the people who obtained full citizenship and the huge numbers of peasants who came to the city seeking work, who could never join a guild and therefore never hold public office, was the main cause of the uprisings. The precarious living conditions of these workers, along with the fact such a large proportion of them were excluded from participation in public office, show how different life could be in the working world of one of the most important cities of the Western world. According to period records, during the 1370s the textile workers feared a return to the economic conditions that had led to the 1345 uprising instigated by Ciuto Brandini. The plague was followed by years of shrinking salaries caused by the gradual rise in prices: the times and the horizons of social change, filled with fear, intolerance and restlessness, became very troubled.

THE REVOLT OF THE CIOMPI (1378)

From the 1350s on, pockets of poverty increased exponentially and the number of *nihil habentes*, the disadvantaged citizens who owned nothing, rose from 66% in 1371 to 73% in 1378. At the beginning of the 1370s, Florence had a population of around 55,000 of whom roughly 13,000 worked in the textile industry. The guild that organized the *ciompi*, the salaried workers involved in the various phases of wool manufacturing, had about 9,000 members. The other two guilds – dyers and doublet-makers – had a total of 4,000, an impressive workforce if we consider the hypothetical total of adult Florentine males.

During the second half of the fourteenth century the entire population of Florence was worn down by exorbitant taxes levied to finance the continuous military campaigns conducted to conquer territory. In addition to the expenses for the annexation of Prato (1350), Pistoia (1351, and definitively conquered in 1401), San Gimignano (1353) and Volterra (1361), and for reinforcing its position in the Mugello and Valdarno districts, in the 1370s the Republic of Florence incurred even more expenses to contain the expansion of the papacy in Tuscany. Even though the pope was exiled in Avignon, the papacy was a dangerous enemy for Florence since it aimed at reestablishing itself in the Papal States by threatening Tuscany, Romagna and the Marches under the able leadership of Cardinal Albornoz. The Republic of Florence, which had sided with the Church against the Empire, rose up against Albornoz and the invasion of the mercenaries led by the English condottiere, John Hawkwood. To combat the papal legate, Florence incited a general uprising of Tuscan and Romagnolo cities that spread quickly and successfully. The war between Florence and the papacy lasted from 1375 to 1378 and was prosecuted by a war council [*balìa*] specially tasked to govern at a particular time. It was made up of eight 'wise' citizens and these Eight Saints skillfully managed the war. Notwithstanding the interdiction – a sort of collective ex-communication – issued against the 'rebel' cities by Pope Gregory XI, and the attempts at mediation of the Dominican mystic, Catherine of Siena, who barely escaped being lynched by the Guelphs, the struggle continued. Not even threats from the Holy Inquisition could stop it: the government of Florence reacted to the attacks from the pope and the Inquisitor by taxing the clergy, making them pay the costs of the war.

This politically and socially unstable climate was the backdrop to the uprising of the *Ciompi*, the wool workers, in 1378. The revolt was triggered by a popular movement that wanted to augment the role of salaried workers within a contradictory and factious working world. The uprising had political causes: it broke out because the heads of the guilds denied citizens of the lower strata their 'right' to representation and participation in the city government. Therefore, notwithstanding Marxist interpretations, the clash between the *popolo grasso* and *popolo minuto* had little in common with the struggle between the developing bourgeoisie and pre-proletariat. The revolt broke out because the number of salaried and unspecialized workers who prepared the wool had increased; they had no political rights, they were paid by the day and they had to submit to the harsh workshop discipline imposed by the *lanifices*, the master wool workers, who had every interest in keeping the multitude of workers on the edges of society.

It was not an alternative between peaceful protests and armed uprising, but between resignation to existing conditions, dictated by fear, and hope for a future change, a hope which – if removed – would transform the men into potential rebels. There were several reasons that prompted the revolts. These included the mundane, such as the need for daily bread, and others that were more ideological, such as the intermittent quest for riches, the aspiration to belong to the governing class and hence to monopolize power. The developments in the phases of the 1378 Revolt of the Ciompi present a perfect picture of how the conflicts in the working world involved forms of government, in this case republican, and how these, governed by the *popolo*, were clearly incapable of guaranteeing social control.

On 18 June 1378, Salvestro de' Medici was elected Gonfalonier of Justice. He submitted a petition to the Signoria proposing the reintroduction of the *Ordinamenti di giustizia*, the laws that the *popolo grasso* had passed against the magnates in 1293. The revival of the struggle between the *popolani* and the magnates sensitized the world of the guilds and, on 21 June, the workers mobilized their militias to hold a demonstration against the Guelph party. The next day a large group of textile and other wage-earning workers as well as immigrants poured into Piazza della Signoria demanding further rules that would strengthen the anti-magnate laws. The infuriated workers rioted in the city streets, attacking buildings and burning and looting the homes of the most prominent members of the Guelph party. One group of insurgents occupied the Stinche Prison and freed all the inmates, then it went to the commune and took over the weapons cache.

During the final days of June, the Ciompi and the members of the minor guilds joined forces, convinced that the merchant and entrepreneurial elites would never agree to substantial concessions. A crowd of several thousand textile workers was ready to gather in front of the Palazzo dei Priori and to attack the home of the Gonfalonier of Justice, Luigi Guicciardini, and the headquarters of the Bailiff who implemented the *Ordinamenti di giustizia*. The rebels captured the *Gonfalone di Giustizia*, the banner that identified the head of the government and was the symbol of his authority. The textile workers planned on eliminating the hated magistrate of the wool guild [*Ufficiale Forestiero dell'Arte della Lana*], to whom the consuls usually delegated the administration of criminal justice and control of the highly composite and restless world of workers. They attacked the guild's headquarters, the Palazzo dell'Arte della Lana, put the Ufficiale Forestiero to flight, and occupied the Palazzo del Podestà where they brutally killed the *Bargello*, Ser Nuto (the *Bargello* was essentially the equivalent of the medieval English 'sheriff' – as of Nottingham, for example).

The uprising spread, and on 22 July the rebels burned the records of the trials of workers and for two days the priors had to remain inside the Palazzo della Signoria, the symbol of local power, until, as recounted by the chronicler Alammano Acciaioli, the rebels finally managed to enter. The government was forced to resign and the results of the previous election were cancelled. The rebels set up a temporary priorate of the guilds that was headed by a wool-guild worker, Michele di Lando and included the members of the two Councils which, in the Florentine Republican system, assisted the supreme magistrate. The new body devoted itself to the program drawn up in a series of secret meetings. Proper implementation of the program was guaranteed by the presence of the revolutionaries' representatives. Over the following days, about thirty members of the Guelph party were exiled. The swashbuckling escape of Lapo di Castiglionchio, a writer accused of siding with the magnates who fled to the Casentino district while his house was looted and burned, is only one of the many stories testifying to the fury of the crowd which, in most cases, summarily executed its enemies in the city's gathering places: the revolutionary court ruled that Lapo be sentenced to death in absentia and that his family be stripped of its civil rights and of the possibility of holding any public office whatsoever.

The rebels created an army of crossbowmen and established three new guilds: the group of those without rights who obtained real citizenship was much bigger than the large group of wool workers. These were the Dyer's Guild [*Arte dei Tintori*], which also included wool workers, carders and soap makers, dryers and menders, makes of tools for textile production and silk weavers; the Doublet-Makers Guild [*Arte dei Farsettai*], which was also open to shearers, tailors, barbers and hatters; and the Guild of the Ciompi, also called the guild of the '*popolo di Dio*', comprising all the wage-earning wool workers – with the teaslers and combers at the fore – along with the weavers. With the community of the guilds remodeled, new criteria for elections were established, with positions equally distributed among the three groups that now comprised the seven major, fourteen minor and three newly-established Florentine Guilds.

The early enthusiasm withered quickly because within just a few weeks it became clear that the new government coalition was contradictory and inadequate, and the institutional boycott of the representatives of the *popolo minuto* was just as evident. It has been calculated that the consequences of the shutdown of wool production put into effect by the workshop owners exposed thousands of workers to unemployment and hunger, that were barely offset by extraordinary measures: the order to all the city's wool manufactories to resume production immediately and to produce at least 2,000 pieces of cloth per month; the loan of a bushel of grain to anyone who requested it; the six-month suspension of the tax on grain and flour; and the reduction of the prices of salt and flour.

The alliance among the various groups of the working world that had spurred the revolt began to waver. Dissatisfaction prompted the workers to radicalize their program, inexorably moving farther away from the more moderate positions of the shopkeepers and artisans, including those who worked in producing wool cloth. Around the end of August, a group of roughly two hundred workers from the Oltrarno district (south of the Arno) met in a field in the Camaldoli neighborhood and decided to resume the initiative on their own. An eight-member committee was created during a crowded assembly held in Piazza San Marco on 27 August. It was given the inspiring name '*Otto Santi della balìa del Popolo di Dio*' [the Eight Saints] – which became an authentic shadow government challenging that in power. The ensuing struggle led to the acceptance of a series of the crowd's demands and to the election of new guild priors. The final clash was soon to come, and on 31 August 1378 the commune's soldiers attacked the insurgents with stones and arrows in Piazza della Signoria, while the guilds' militias attacked the wool workers and forced them to retreat with serious losses. On 1 September 1378, a specially-called general parliament abolished the Arte dei Ciompi and all the prerogatives and rights connected to its existence.

The uprising failed to achieve its goals, but it does shed light on the limitations of the government of the *popolo* that ruled the city from 1282 and would, through various vicissitudes, govern it as an oligarchy until it became a principality in 1530. The rebels' demands during the Revolt of the Ciompi highlight the weakness of the political dynamics within the Florentine republican system and reveal the people's inability to achieve domestic political cohesion. This lack of cohesion can be placed within a more general, endemic inability on the part of the political actors to define and develop a shared political language during any phase of the history of the Florentine Republic.

THE OLIGARCHIC GOVERNMENT (1378-1434)

From 1378 to 1434 Florence was governed by a mercantile oligarchy which, with the participation of the followers of the fourteenth century's intellectual giants, Dante, Boccaccio and Petrarch, allowed Florence to become the center of Humanism and to become fully aware of its political, intellectual, artistic and economic importance. The Florentine republican system was based on *Consulte e Pratiche*, documents containing the results of the government's consultative and legislative sessions. The *Libri Fabarum* were crucially important: books in which the administrations recorded votes for and against each proposed law. The laws that were passed were entered in the *Provvisioni*, the permanent body of the republic's laws.

During the fourteenth century, the political representation of the popular base increased exponentially and, even though it would never be fully democratic because the minorities were always excluded from holding public office, in 1343, 10% of 3,000 candidates were certified as electable to the highest offices. In 1363 the number of eligible citizens rose to 500, and in 1382, 750 of the 5,000 candidates' names were put into the bags [*borse*] from which the names of the representatives of public offices were drawn. These were exceptional results compared to the other European governments of the time, which were mostly absolute monarchies.

However, even though the number of eligible citizens grew exponentially, power always remained in the hands of the main families, of the *popolo grasso*, who shared it based on agreements among their heads. Maso degli Albizi, Gino Capponi and Niccolò da Uzzano defined the city's political orientation. They represented a limited group of families who, through their 'friendships', kept the government in their hands by controlling the contents of the *borse* from which the names of the priors were drawn by lot. This process led to the establishment of an oligarchic regime in which a small fraction of the people governed Florence exclusively for about forty years. During the fifteenth century, this procedure led to an oblique road to power for one person, beginning with Maso degli Albizi (1343-1417) and continuing in 1417 with his son, Rinaldo (1370-1442), through a hereditary succession that highlights a single dominant family's rise to power, as would later happen with the Medici.

In the same period, the city continued to pursue its expansionistic aims in Tuscany. Florence fought expensive wars against Arezzo, Cortona and Pisa, which were conquered and annexed between the end of the fourteenth century and the beginning of the fifteenth. The conquest of Pisa in 1406 was of vital importance for Florence because it allowed the city's merchants to stop using ports such as Seville and Lisbon. Now the Florentine companies could access the sea directly from Pisa.

The oligarchy also opposed the claims of the Visconti, the dukes of Milan who controlled most of the Po Valley and had every intention of extending their domains to central Italy. The war between the Florentine Republic and the Duchy of Milan ended on 8 February 1420 and enabled the Florentine humanist chancellor, Coluccio Salutati (1331-1406), a pupil of Petrarch, and Leonardo Bruni (1370-1444), translator, philosopher, scholar and Salutati's successor, to proclaim Florence as the home of liberty and heir to Rome. Rome's symbolic value had remained unchanged over the centuries, even though the Eternal City had been reduced to a town with little authority. The popes were still living in Avignon – politically controlled by the king of France – and from 1374 to 1417 the Great Schism set the cardinals against each other in the papal election, resulting in the presence of a pope and an antipope, a division that damaged Saint Peter's throne in terms of both spiritual importance and economic recovery.

Therefore, while Rome was spiritually and intellectually weak, Florence was the homeland of the three founders of humanism, Dante, Petrarch and Boccaccio, and the flourishing center of arts and letters of the entire known world. The frescoes by Masaccio (1401-1428), the first painter to use linear perspective, the statues by Donatello (1386-1466), the most 'experimental' of fifteenth-century sculptors and, above all, the great dome by Filippo Brunelleschi (1377-1446), built between 1420 and 1436, proved that the 'City of the Lily' was truly the intellectual and artistic capital of Christendom. The citizens of the Republic of Florence participated in public affairs and kept the city's intellectual level high: men of culture participated in political life so that the republic was led by the best citizens in a way that justified and authorized the oligarchy.

The city's rise to riches crystallized around Giovanni di Bicci de' Medici (1360-1429), the head of the most powerful Calimala company that had branches in all of the world's markets and financed popes and princes. Giovanni's financial success was evident from the weight his family brought to bear in the commune's councils. And although he was not the richest man in the city, his possessions gave him enormous power over the government of the rich Florentine merchants.

On 22 May 1427, the Republic of Florence decreed a new tax survey and assessment: the *Catasto*, which established the basis on which citizens would pay taxes from that time on. Each citizen had to inform the authorities of his name and the names, ages and occupations of each of his family members, the real estate and movable property owned within and without the Florentine domains, amounts of money, credits, trade dealings, merchandise, oxen, horses, flocks and herds. The *Catasto* made it very clear that if anyone concealed assets they would be confiscated. The system required the payment of 10 *soldi* for every 100 florins so it was progressive taxation: below 100 florins one paid an average of 3% of the declared income, and above 100 florins the rate was 5%.

The 1427 *Catasto* did not meet with the Medici family's approval. On more than one occasion the Medici expressed reserves about its underlying principles and the fact that the taxes were used to finance the war against Milan, which they opposed. Furthermore, the new system weighed on the families of the *popolo* since the most heavily taxed wealth consisted mainly of movable assets.

The *Catasto* of 1427 shows that Giovanni di Bicci de' Medici was the second wealthiest citizen after Palla Strozzi. With nearly 163,000 florins of gross assets and 101,000 florins of net assets after the deductions allowed by law, Messer Palla was by far the richest taxpayer in Florence. Giovanni di Bicci de' Medici was second with a net wealth of 79,000 florins, a sum that was equal to the annual earnings of 2,000 workers with an average salary of 40 florins a year. So, even though he was not the richest man in Florence, Giovanni did have enormous wealth.

The rules of the *Catasto* included a series of tax reliefs and deductions that only the richest taxpayers – such as Giovanni di Bicci –

could use. There was a deduction of 200 florins for each dependent – children, wives, servants – that the head of the family supported. Furthermore, the family home was not included in the calculation of taxable assets and quite frequently the 'home' was a palace or a group of adjacent and connecting houses. A rich merchant like Giovanni could also deduct all debts to third parties, the costs of maintaining industrial facilities such as dyeing and drying shops, fulling mills, mills and hotels, as well as the depreciation of infrastructure and the animals used in farm work.

If Giovanni di Bicci de' Medici was not the 'first citizen' in terms of wealth, he certainly was in terms of approval. This was mainly because he came from a family whose ancestors included Salvestro de' Medici, who had supported the *popolo* during the Revolt of the Ciompi in 1378 despite the fact that he belonged to a family that acquired its enormous wealth from banking.

The early years of the fifteenth century were marked by the rivalry between the noble Albizi and the Medici who came from common stock. The most dangerous and powerful of the Albizi was Rinaldo, whose single goal was to modify the taxation system in order to regain popularity among his peers. He aimed at having the highest taxes imposed on movable assets since this would penalize the *popolo* families whose riches came from trade. However, the funeral held for Giovanni di Bicci on 20 February 1429, attended by representatives of the German emperor and dignitaries from the Republic of Venice, bore witness to the power the Medici had acquired in the city. The baton was passed to Giovanni's firstborn son, Cosimo (1389-1434), a man who was as skilled in business and prudent in politics as his father.

Rinaldo degli Albizi lost credibility with the Florentine people for having wanted the very costly war against Lucca and achieving nothing more than a slightly profitable peace in 1433. But he did succeed in asking for his rival's head by accusing him of not having been capable of negotiating the peace settlement with the city of San Donato. However, the judiciary merely declared Cosimo a magnate, sentencing him to exclusion from all positions in the city after a brief imprisonment in the Alberghetto, the cell in Arnolfo's tower of the Palazzo dei Priori. In September 1433, Cosimo was exiled to Padua for ten years, but the city that was under the rule of Venice welcomed him with open arms, and princely honors. Rinaldo could not destroy his political rival who, while abroad had transferred his business to the Veneto region and became the leader of the adversaries of the government headed by Rinaldo degli Albizi.

The gonfalonier and the majority of the priors elected between September and October 1434 backed Cosimo: on 29 September 1434 the parliament revoked the sentence against him and declared him not a magnate. Cosimo returned to Florence on 5 October 1434. The cheers with which he was welcomed – masterfully depicted in a fresco by Giorgio Vasari (1511-1574) in the room named for Cosimo in Palazzo della Signoria – made him the master of the city without his ever having held any political office.

THE MEDICI (1434-1494)

Cosimo de' Medici had all the requisites for establishing a *signoria*, the authoritarian form of government Florence was evolving towards on its own. He was still a Florentine among the many, a citizen who lived in a very beautiful palace – but not the most beautiful of all – in the city: Palazzo Medici on Via Larga built by the architect Michelozzo, born Michelozzo di Bartolomeo Michelozzi (1396-1472), who drew his inspiration from Filippo Brunelleschi's models. Cosimo led a comfortable, but not excessively lavish life. He held posts in the city's main magistracies only for a six-month period, but he secured his dominance through a large circle of friends, surrounding himself with a group of loyal men including Luca Pitti and Tommaso Soderini, whose names, along with many others, were drawn by lots in the city's elections to public offices. The primary goal of the Medici regime was to control election procedures, specifically the appointment of the *Accoppiatori* who chose the names of the *imborsati*, from whom the members of the Signoria, the government's executive body, were elected. The *imborsati* were electable citizens whose names were put into the bags [*borse*] from which the slips of paper with the names of the eligible men were drawn. Controlling this system, by making sure that only the names of his friends and those loyal to him were in the bags, made it possible for Cosimo not to enter the government but to control who was elected to the city's public offices. Now, only persons connected to him could be part of the government, fueling and gradually enlarging the circle of his 'party's' supporters.

The regime established in Florence in the fall of 1434 did not overturn the republican balance of Florentine identity and maintained intact the constitutional arrangement of the communal era. From the previous coalition led by the Albizi family it inherited a consolidated power system which, in turn, adapted to the new political contingencies of the city and the surroundings without ever losing its original proto-democratic identity. A great businessman, Cosimo de' Medici personally controlled all the companies of which he was the main partner and this skill, coupled with prudence, enabled him to double his personal wealth within a very short time.

Cosimo associated the image of his family with the cult of the Magi and he masked the lavishness of his secret power as he walked through the city streets on the Feast of the Epiphany. This cult had been rooted in Florence since the last decade of the fourteenth century and was spread throughout the city by the Dominican friars of San Marco. Cosimo took one of Christianity's founding rituals and transformed it into a tool for obtaining the citizenry's political approval by associating the Medici forever with the three pagan kings who, by their visit, rendered homage to the new Christian king. By financing each celebration related to this cult, Cosimo appropriated a metaphor that permitted the Medici to indicate their political epiphany through the religious celebration, consolidating the perception that the Florentines had of them as guarantors of the common weal, as builders of secular structures, builders and restorers of parishes and churches and founders of academies and libraries. What other direct and effective message could be used to convey to the Florentines that the Medici were good and respectful Christians?

In the early years of the fifteenth century, ever closer contacts with ancient civilization and thinking aroused new curiosities among men who were increasingly rationally focused on responding to questions concerning the secrets of nature and their own identity as men. Painting was one of the tools of rational research used to seek answers to these questions: in 1420 the architect Filippo Brunelleschi invented perspective – a way of depicting three-dimensional space on the two-dimensional surface of a panel or wall – and this technique gave man a more precise awareness of reality and a more effective dominion over nature.

Patronage, typical of rich Florentines in the fourteenth century, continued ceaselessly during the fifteenth: the support of the wealth and interest of merchant families made for very lavish artistic commissions. Gradually this large-scale production of art objects and architecture led to the appearance of a new type of man, a man who, by emulating the ancients, tried to elevate himself, embodying virtues such as moral courage, intelligence, encyclopedic intelligence, aptitude for all the arts and the ability to excel in many fields. The first representative of this typically Florentine genius and spirit was the writer, painter, architect, sculptor, and philosopher, Leon Battista Alberti (1404-1472).

Cosimo de' Medici was an expert in business and diplomacy. He turned his interest in art and philosophy into politics by choosing architecture, painting and sculpture as the perfect means of communication for creating approval for his family. Cosimo was a patron and, as such, he continued what his father had begun. Giovanni had commissioned Filippo Brunelleschi to build the sacristy in San Lorenzo along with vestries and rooms for the canons and his own burial chapel. When the family palazzo was built on Via Larga, adjacent to Piazza San Lorenzo, the basilica became the Medici family's parish and the thousand-year-old early Christian church, which was in terrible condition, was entirely rebuilt at Cosimo's expense to plans by Filippo Brunelleschi who was at the same time engaged in building the dome of Santa Maria del Fiore. Then, Cosimo had a group of Dominican friars transferred to the same district that was becoming the fulcrum of the family's wealth and generosity. Cosimo financed the new convent for the friars which was built by Michelozzo and frescoed by Fra' Giovanni Angelico, one of the resident brothers. Vespasiano da Bisticci (1421-1498), was the most famous *stationarius* of the Italian Renaissance. A book merchant and owner of a workshop that produced manuscripts, he devoted a long section of the *Vita di Cosimo de' Medici* to celebrating his illustrious fellow citizen as an enlightened promoter of art and culture. The biography highlighted Cosimo's generosity, his moral rectitude, his constant service on behalf of the city and dwelt on the public works he sponsored, on the huge sums he donated for the construction of religious buildings (churches and convents inside and outside Florence), for the establishment of the libraries of the convents of San Marco and the Badia Fiesolana as well as for the restoration and rebuilding of San Lorenzo. To keep the emphasis on Cosimo's public works, Vespasiano only touched on the construction of the palazzo on Via Larga and the villas at Careggi and Cafaggiolo – the family's private residences – without writing a word about their beauty and importance. The author concluded the description of Cosimo's building projects and opened the last section of the *Vita* by praising his wisdom and culture and describing his generous deeds. With a very clear message, Vespasiano reminds the reader that even the private projects were proof of Cosimo's munificence because they created jobs for Florentines and therefore had a positive effect on the entire community. On 6 July 1439, under the auspices of the Medici, the papal bull *Laetentur Coeli* (*Let the Heavens Rejoice*) was read in the cathedral of Santa Maria del Fiore. The bull, issued by Pope Eugene IV, announced the reunification of the Roman Catholic Church and the Eastern Orthodox Churches, ending the schism between them. The council, which had been moved from Ferrara to Florence at Cosimo's instigation, achieved its goal, even if only on paper.

When he died in 1464, Cosimo was interred in the pillar supporting the transept in the church of San Lorenzo, signifying – both symbolically and physically – that one of the most important basilicas in Florence was supported by the generous donations of its patron. On the marker indicating the place of Cosimo's interment, he is called *Pater patriae*, the same title that the Romans bestowed on victorious military leaders.

Piero the Gouty (1416-1469) was his sole surviving son, who owed the nickname to the disease caused by excessive consumption of meat, which was common among the rich and powerful. Although he specialized in business, he *de facto* inherited his father's position in the political and financial dynamics of the Republic of Florence. Piero continued the process of concentrating Medici power using the crisis that followed the conspiracy led by the so-called *fazione del Poggio*. It was 1466 and Piero discovered a plot against his family organized by Luca Pitti (who had been a friend of his father Cosimo), Angelo Acciaiuoli, and Niccolò Soderini. The plotters were all exiled except for Dietisalvi Neroni, the last of them, who was captured near Prato and put to death by hanging which Piero wanted done in public so that it could be witnessed by and serve as an example to all.

In order to prevent the spread of dissent against the Republic of Florence, Piero de' Medici increasingly put his family at the center of the state through every public event and occasion. There are many examples of this strategy, not the least of which was the tournament of 7 January 1469 held in Piazza Santa Croce in honor of his son: it was an opportunity to emphasize the Medici's superiority over their rivals. There were many voices of dissent, one belonged to the republican Donato Giannotti who expressed his deep concern about the abundance of symbols and arms that 'are all things that diminish the public's reputation, and increase [it] for private [individuals]'

(*sono tutte cose che tolgono riputazione al pubblico, ed accrescionla a'
privati*).

It was also part of his quest for approval that Piero arranged for the
marriage of his firstborn, Lorenzo with the noble lady from Rome, Cla-
rice Orsini (1453-1488). They were married by proxy in Rome on 10
December 1468, and the official wedding date was set for 4 June 1469,
in Florence, with four days of festivities. By giving his son a foreign
wife, from one of the most influential noble families in Rome, Piero
made a political choice that was not very popular among the Florentines,
but strengthened his contacts in Rome where the most profitable branch
of the bank was located and where being related to one of the oldest
and most influential families in that city could make a huge difference.

When Piero died in 1469, he left two young sons, Lorenzo (1449-
1492) and Giuliano (1453-1478). For obvious reasons, it was the firstborn who succeeded him as head of the republic. A terrible
businessman, Lorenzo let the companies in London and Bruges decline and they both failed in 1478. Exactly ten years later, the Lyon
company also wavered because he was incapable of controlling the
financial dynamics caused by the poor management of the director,
Francesco Sassetti (1421-1490). Lorenzo conceived his role as a statesman and his private life as a work of art. He surrounded himself with
humanists and scholars such as Marsilio Ficino, Angelo Poliziano
and Pico della Mirandola; he thrived on the philosophical discussions
he listened to at the Academy he established at Careggi, turning to
ancient models for finding a solution to the spiritual, intellectual and
moral problems of his day.

Notwithstanding his lack of ability in managing business, Lorenzo
– known as the Magnificent because of his passion for the arts – was
extremely adept in political strategy and skillfully strengthened the
family's power over the republic. This was borne out by the effects of
the revolt that broke out in the Prato – a city within the Florentine
domains – in 1470. After the revolt he succeeded in creating a limited
Grand Council, tasked with controlling the Council of One Hundred,
which was the last bulwark defending the city's republican practices
and institutions. Creating a Grand Council was the *de facto* establishment of a parallel government that allowed the Medici to dominate
the city's politics. The war he waged against Volterra in 1472 led to
Florence's conquest of the city and its alum mines, an essential material for Florentine textile production.

However, during those years, several political powers harbored aspirations to the Florentine territory, including Volterra. Not least among these was Pope Sixtus IV (born Francesco della Rovere) who wanted to take over the rich Florentine dominions to finance the costly works he had started in Rome, such as the embellishment and reorganization of the Vatican library, and to promote the careers of his nephews, including Girolamo Riario. The pope did not look kindly on the Medici's expansionist aims in Romagna and had already shown his hostility by ousting them from the administration of the papacy's finances and replacing them with a rival family of Florentine bankers, the Pazzi.

The Pazzi Conspiracy was engineered by the rival family to crack the Medici hegemony, and supported by the pope, the duke of Urbino, and the archbishop of Pisa, along with others who looked on from a distance because they stood to gain from the collapse of the Medici in Florence. The assault took place on 26 April 1478, when Giuliano de' Medici was brutally killed in the cathedral of Santa Maria del Fiore. However, the plot failed because Lorenzo the Magnificent, who was only wounded, survived by hiding in the cathedral sacristy.

In the dramatic backlash to the plot, all the members of the Pazzi family were killed, hanged from the windows of the Palazzo dei Priori. Having eliminated his most violent enemies, Lorenzo seized the opportunity to reinforce his personal power by creating a Council of Seventy. He chose the members himself and delegated basic powers, in particular the election of the Priors (1480). In 1490 he concentrated this power in an even smaller, hence even more docile, council of just seventeen members. There was no longer any need to turn to the parliament, since these small councils were permanent special committees with executive powers. In order to control them in the most efficient and direct way possible, Lorenzo had himself elected to the councils of Seventy and Seventeen, so that he could intervene in the decision-making dynamics of the government of the Florentine Republic without any opposition. He also strengthened his powers in foreign policy, becoming the scale-tipper of Italian policy, the arbiter who prevented Venice from turning to the king of France, who was a heir of the Angevins and related to the Visconti family. Finally, in 1489, Lorenzo even obtained the cardinal's hat for his son, Giovanni. This was the birth of a true dynasty.

The repression of dissent under Lorenzo's rule became public spectacle. It was realized maintaining a tone at once official, since it was directly expressed by the bodies that held power, and secular, since it was separate and independent of the operation of the religious and ecclesiastic system. Under Lorenzo, banishment and the obligation to live outside the commune were no longer used to repress political dissent. They had become the legacy of the early commune's struggles. Instead, the death penalty, which was much more effective because of its spectacular nature, became the preferred method for resolving political conflict, the ideal instrument for quelling dissent.

The powerful images, combined with the words and gestures connected with the death penalty, were now projected directly onto the public. The coats of arms of the judges, like the symbolic sites for announcing the sentences and carrying out the executions, transformed the final procession of the condemned person, cleverly routed through the city's most important streets, into a sort of lay 'passion'. Passing through the city's symbolic sites where the convict was quartered and his body displayed, the result was a psychodrama in which the sole, negative hero was the condemned man himself.

When Lorenzo died in 1492, the baton passed to his son Piero (1472-1503), known as 'the Unfortunate' who succeeded him in a situation that was far from promising. The ruin of the Medici companies culminated in bankruptcy in 1494, leaving Piero without personal capital, while the Dominican preacher, Frà Girolamo Savonarola (1452-1498) stirred up the city against the Medici, hoping to transform Florence into a new Jerusalem, ready to purify itself of the sins of the Renaissance. Savonarola's fiery sermons shook the intellectual and moral foundations of the Medici regime.

The invasion of Italy by King Charles VIII of France threw the entire peninsula into turmoil. In 1494, by agreeing to an alliance with the invader and taking that crucial decision without consulting the Signoria, Piero betrayed the city's true spirit and its innate desire for freedom. Many of his supporters abandoned him. Piero was driven from Florence on 9 November 1494, his palace was looted and Lorenzo the Magnificent's unfortunate son became the symbol of his family's decline as it fell into ruin.

Andrea da Firenze, *Path to Salvation*, 1365-67, Spanish Chapel, Santa Maria Novella, Florence.

Leonardo da Vinci, *Annunciation*, 1472 ca., the Uffizi Gallery, Florence.

Michelangelo Buonarroti (1475-1564), *David* (1501-1504), the Accademia Gallery, Florence.

Michelangelo Buonarroti, *Bandini Pietà*, Museo dell'Opera del Duomo, Florence.

Fra' Carnevale (attribution), *The Ideal City*, 1490s. Walters Art Gallery, Baltimore.

Bernardo Bellotto (1720-1780), *The Piazza della Signoria in Florence* (1740), Szépmûvészeti Múseum, Budapest.

Pompeo Batoni, *Pietro Leopoldo, Granduca di Toscana, e il fratello Giuseppe II Imperatore durante un soggiorno a Roma*, particular, 1769, oil on canvas, Kunsthistorisches Museum, Vienna.

Enrico Fanfani (1824-post 1885), *The Arrival of Vittorio Emanuele II in Piazza della Signoria of Florence* (1861), Private collection.

G.A. Van Wittel (Gaspare Vanvitelli), *The Arno at the Cascine*, oil on canvas, Florence, Collection of the entity *Cassa di Risparmio* of Florence.

The elegant profile of the Leopolda station in a drawing by Enrico Presenti (The Historic Archive of the Comune di Firenze, *Fondi disegni*, 359/8).

La Loggia of the Signoria in Florence in a photograph by Giorgio Sommer in 1871 ca., Milan, Private collection.

Public Stadium "Artemio Franchi" (1929-1932), Florence, designed by: Nervi
Pierluigi, Giuntoli Alessandro.

Florence, the Chain Map. Florence in XV century with the walls concluded in 1333 represented in the so-called *Carta della Catena*.

Piazza Santa Croce during the 1966 flood.

Ruins of the Ponte Santa Trinita, August 1944.

Mod. 3

COMUNE DI FIRENZE

5 novembre 1966

IL SINDACO

Visto l'art. 4 del Decreto Presidenziale 15 giugno
1959 n. 393 Testo Unico delle norme sulla circolazione stradale;
Considerata la grave situazione determinatasi in se
guito all'alluvione nella zona del Lungarno Corsini, Lungarno
Archibusieri, Lungarno delle Grazie, per il crollo delle spal
lette del fiume Arno e nel Lungarno Acciaioli per il crollo di
parte della carreggiata;
Considerato altresì lo stato di pericolosità determi
natosi nella zona sopraddetta per l'eventualità di possibili
crolli, in particolare nel Lungarno Acciaioli;
Ritenuto pertanto, a tutela della pubblica incolumità,
di vietare la circolazione agli automezzi privati nella zona
suddetta;

ORDINA

che sia vietata la circolazione agli automezzi privati nella
zona delimitata dai Lungarni Corsini, Acciaioli, Archibusieri,
Medici, Piazza dei Giudici, Lungarni Diaz e delle Grazie, Piaz
za Cavalleggeri, Lungarno della Zecca Vecchia, Via Tripoli
(esclusa), Corso dei Tintori (escluso), Via Malenchini (esclusa)
come pure esclusi Piazza Mentana, Via dei Saponai, Piazza dei
Giudici, Via dei Castellani, Via della Ninna, Piazzale degli Uf
fizi, Via Lambertesca, Borgo SS. Apostoli, Piazza S. Trinita,
Via del Parione.

*One of the first ordinances issued by Mayor Piero Bargellini, the day after the 4th
of November* (From a press release of the Commune of Florence – special file
in the care of the Press Office of the Commune, 1965-68).

Piazza del Duomo at 10:00 on November 4th submersed in water. The cathedral, the bell tower of Giotto, and the Baptistery are surrounded like rocks engulfed by a stormy sea. The precious baptistery door, the one at the south by Andrea Pisano, the on at the north and the famous door of Paradise by Lorenzo Ghiberti, become literally flogged from logs and from household goods transported by the flood. The flooded streets are also by now full of torrents that reverse with a furry in the piazza, forming frightening whirlpools at every intersection.

Anton Hautmann, *A stroll in Via Dei Calzaioli, Florence*, 1862 circa; albumen print on paper, part of stereoscopy, 8x8. Hautmann Archive, Florence.

11.

From the Republic to the Principality (1494-1530)

With Piero di Lorenzo de' Medici's ruin and banishment, the history of the Republic of Florence became involved in the widespread upheavals affecting the Italian peninsula between the end of the fifteenth century and the first two decades of the sixteenth. The ambitions of the kings of France to acquire more territory in Italy reignited and complicated the struggles between the papacy and the empire. The Duchy of Milan and the Republic of Venice, the most important city-states of the north, participated in the clashes. In the meantime, Florentine bankers continued lending money to the kings of France and promoting their business beyond the Alps, influencing the city's politics which, in that period, were pro-French.

Politically, Florence was divided between those who wanted Piero de' Medici to return and the mass of citizens of every social class who, perturbed by Savonarola's mystical and prophetic sermons, were convinced that the French conquest was punishment for the fifteenth century's neo-paganism and decadence. On 7 February 1497, which was Shrove Tuesday, the Dominican friar's followers did not hesitate to throw their silk finery, valuable objects and the magnificent paintings they had purchased at great cost from the artists of the day, into a bonfire of the vanities lit in the middle of Piazza della Signoria. The objective of this destructive fury was to eliminate any item that could be considered a symbol of vanity and therefore potentially sinful.

By this time Savonarola was informally the head of the Florentine Republic and, at his suggestion, a new constitution was drafted, based on the Venetian model, entrusting the principal political role to a Grand Council, comprising members of the city's leading families. The *Salone dei Cinquecento*, the new seat of the parliament was built, expanding the Palazzo dei Priori towards the east.

The Dominican friar continued to preach from the pulpit of the church of San Marco, inveighing against the pope and the papal court that, in his opinion, lived in splendor, and against those Florentines who were inclined to live in luxury and favored the restoration of the Medici. The clash with Pope Alexander VI culminated when the pontiff prohibited Savonarola from preaching and ordered the Florentine Republic to deliver up the friar to him. The Dominican tried to restore his power over the Florentines by announcing a 'trial by fire'. He was ready to walk through flames to prove his divine inspiration. But he wavered and delayed before the crowd that had gathered in Piazza della Signoria to witness the miracle. It was 7 April 1498 and luckily enough, weather interrupted the event as rain poured down on the square putting out the flames and saving Florence from a possible riot due to loss of faith in their prophet. The chronicler Luca Landucci wrote: '... during a great thunderstorm and rough weather amidst driving rain and a disturbance of the elements. I happen to remember it as I got soaked through when I went to see the trial by fire, because it was on that day about 20 in the evening'. Savonarola was arrested on orders from the Signoria and was handed over to the Inquisition that condemned him and two of his disciples as heretics and turned them over to the secular court. So, on 23 May 1498, Girolamo Savonarola and the other two Dominican friars were burned alive in Piazza Signoria and their ashes were scattered in the Arno.

The city was in the midst of a great political crisis: the revolt by Pisa dragged Florence into an expensive and difficult fifteen-year war that ended only in 1509 with Pisa's definitive subjugation. During those violent and bloody years, the influential Florentines tried to stabilize the government by establishing a magistracy, once again inspired by the Republic of Venice. Like the doge in the Most Serene Republic, in 1502 the position of Gonfalonier of Justice was extended to a lifetime term. Piero Soderini (1450-1522), a member of an old Florentine family and once close to the Piero the Unfortunate, was appointed to the post.

In 1504 the symbol of Florence's rediscovered freedom from tyranny was erected to protect the Palazzo della Signoria. The colossal statue of *David* that Michelangelo carved in just three years protected the Republic's independence. The position, selected by a special committee, 'turned' the gaze of the Biblical hero preparing for the battle with Goliath threateningly to the south, that is towards Rome. In this same period Piero Soderini decided to have the walls of the Salone dei Cinquecento in Palazzo della Signoria decorated with frescoes.

He commissioned Michelangelo and Leonardo da Vinci to depict the two battles in which Florence preserved its liberty: the Battle of Cascina, fought against Pisa on 29 July 1364 and the Battle of Anghiari between the Florentine and Milanese armies on 29 June 1440. Michelangelo prepared a grandiose cartoon, but never started the painting because he left Florence for Rome on invitation from Pope Julius II. Leonardo, after having unsuccessfully experimented with a new technique – mixing pigments with wax – abandoned the project in defeat and moved to France.

Notwithstanding Soderini's efforts, Niccolò Machiavelli (1469-1527), the chancellor of the Republic of Florence and founder of political science, stressed the need to establish a state headed by a powerful prince capable of acting against the increasingly centralized forces of neighboring states. In the meantime, the humanists continued to devote themselves to the personal quest for truth, to criticism, to the studying the texts containing the ideas of the ancients, both pagans and Christians. In 1513, Machiavelli wrote the treatise on political doctrine, *De Principatibus* (*On Principalities*), subsequently entitled *The Prince*. In twenty-six chapters, the author set out the characteristics of an ideal prince and the methods for conquering and maintaining power.

Towards the end of the fifteenth century, the Florentine financier, navigator and cartographer Amerigo Vespucci (1454-1512), who had worked for the Medici agency in Seville, applied the doctrine of the Florentine cosmographers to the voyages of the Genoese navigator, Christopher Columbus. The Spanish Crown appointed him to explore the southern coasts of the continent Columbus had reached. Thus, in two consecutive voyages, in 1499 and 1501-1502, Vespucci proved that the lands the Genoese navigator had found were not the Indies, but a New World which, the cartographer Martin Waldseemüller (1470-1521) named 'America' in his honor in 1507.

Notwithstanding the achievements of these men, Florence was gradually ceding its position as the center of Renaissance innovation and research to Rome which, thanks to the patronage of the popes and of the rich cardinals' families, was the most important center of cultural production in Christendom throughout the entire sixteenth century. However, certain Florentines also contributed to this: before dying, Lorenzo the Magnificent assured the future of the Medici's domination of Florence by having his son Giovanni (1475-1521) made a cardinal. Elected pope in 1513, with the name Leo X, he became both Lord of the Church and Lord of Florence, guaranteeing the family's return to the city. But, even though Leo placed the papacy's resources at the service of the Medici, during his pontificate Florence became an appendage of the Papal States. Leo X governed both territories, but was always far from his home city and, in a society where power existed when it was visible, the distance made the difference and led to another inevitable loss of the Medici's power over the city. Under Leo X, Medici power in Florence was exercised by his nephew – Piero's son – Lorenzo, whom the pope made Duke of Urbino. Lorenzo died suddenly in 1518 and was replaced by his cousin Giulio (1478-1534), created cardinal by Leo X. When Giuliano, Duke of Nemours, died in 1516, there were no more legitimate male descendants of Lorenzo the Magnificent.

Leo X died in 1521: after the short papacy of Alexander VI, Giulio de' Medici was elected to the papal seat in 1523 and took the name Clement VII. The government in Florence was run by cardinal Passerini from Cortona on behalf of Alessandro and Ippolito, the two illegitimate sons of Giuliano, Duke of Nemours, and the last descendants of Lorenzo the Magnificent. To celebrate a dynasty that seemed to be approaching its end, Pope Clement VII commissioned Michelangelo to build a grandiose funerary monument against the transept of San Lorenzo: a chapel mirroring the sacristy where Giovanni di Bicci was interred in 1429. The new chapel honored the two recently-deceased dukes, Lorenzo, Duke of Urbino, and Giuliano, Duke of Nemours, as well as the two 'Magnificent' men, Giuliano and Lorenzo who died in 1478 and 1492, respectively. The project, which was left unfinished when Michelangelo left definitively for Rome in 1534, is proof not only of the artist's brilliance as an architect and sculptor, but also of his difficult relationship with the sixteenth-century Medici.

These were not easy years for the Medici family: Clement VII had dragged Florence into a hostile and nearsighted policy against Charles V of Habsburg (1500-1588), Holy Roman Emperor and king of Spain. After devastating Rome in the sack of 6 May 1527, the imperial troops headed towards Florence while the city rose up in the name of liberty, banished the Medici and restored a regime similar to that suggested by Savonarola. Niccolò Capponi (1472-1529), who descended from two of the most important and traditionally influential families in fifteenth-century Florentine politics, was elected Gonfalonier of Justice for one year and proclaimed Jesus Christ king of Florence. But the new regime did not survive the pope's reconciliation with the emperor: according to the 1529 Treaty of Bologna, the Medici returned to Florence and Alessandro (1510-1537), introduced as the son of the Duke of Urbino but perhaps, as rumored in the city, the illegitimate son of Pope Clement VII himself, was elevated to the rank of duke.

The siege of Florence (1529-1530) by the imperial troops was the final act of Spanish domination in Italy by Charles V. The Republic of Florence resisted the imperial and papal armies for eleven months but was forced to surrender on 12 August 1530. The Medici established a monarchy that had nothing in common with the fifteenth-century version which, at least formally, respected the republican system. Now the government of Florence was based on monarchical principles; the commune had failed and the republic's identity was rubbed out: the liberty that had inspired the city during the governments of the *popolo* was literally erased from its vocabulary. Florence acclaimed Alessandro de' Medici as the first Duke of Florence. And yet, the fame of distinguished figures such as Filippo Strozzi, Amerigo Vespucci, Giovanni da Verrazano, Michelangelo Buonarroti, Niccolò Machiavelli, and Francesco Guicciardini was not sufficient to hide the political transition that had taken place in Florence. Florence was no longer a free republic: it was a principality controlled by one man alone.

THE GRAND DUCHY OF TUSCANY (1530-1737)

The emperor made Alessandro de' Medici Duke of Florence in 1532 and he held the title until 1537. During his reign, he proceeded to gradually dismantle the Florentine republican institutions which were definitively transformed in an absolutistic key by Cosimo I de' Medici (1537-1574), his distant cousin and successor to the government of the city. Under Alessandro's rule, the Florentine institutions maintained a vague semblance of democracy through the Grand Council of Two Hundred (*Gran Consiglio dei Duecento*) and the Senate, composed of forty-eight members appointed for life with advisory powers. In actual fact, Alessandro held the executive power and impressed a typical princely character on his government, depriving all the institutions that had controlled the city during the communal period of their power and meaning. He began with the guilds, which had been an important part of the communal city-state's political system since 1282 but now no longer had any role. The new duke allied himself with Europe's greatest reigning families and, through the intervention of his uncle, Pope Clement VII, he was able to marry one of Charles V's illegitimate daughters and then, in 1533, marry off his stepsister Caterina, the legitimate daughter of Lorenzo, Duke of Urbino, to Henry, Duke of Orléans, the second son of King Francis I of France.

Alessandro had lived at Charles V's imperial court and brought some of its customs back to Florence. He surrounded himself with a guard of lansquenets, German soldiers. Armed with halberds, they frightened and disconcerted the Florentines who were accustomed to seeing even the most authoritarian Medici behave with more discretion. In line with the increasingly 'princely' nature of the new government, Alessandro eliminated the symbols of the republican and communal institutions that were so dear to the Florentines. One of the most significant of these actions was certainly his appointment of the sculptor Benvenuto Cellini to make new coins, different from the florin and bearing his portrait. Furthermore, Alessandro demanded that private citizens surrender their weapons to him. The death of Pope Clement VII in 1534 weakened the duke's power and a group of dissidents led by Filippo Strozzi tried to restore liberty in the city and overthrow Alessandro's regime. During the night of 6 January 1537, Alessandro was assassinated by his cousin, Lorenzino de' Medici, (called Lorenzaccio) from the branch of the family that descended from Cosimo the Elder's brother.

It was Cosimo the Younger, who belonged to the cadet branch of the Medici family – son of the condottiere Giovanni dale Bande Nere (1498-1526) and related to Lorenzo the Magnificent only on his mother's side – who took advantage of Alessandro's death. Since Alessandro died childless, Cosimo managed to have himself appointed as Duke of Florence in 1537 at the age of seventeen. In the eyes of many influential Florentines, his youth and his modest demeanor made him appear weak, superficial and only interested in women, so that he appeared easy to influence and manipulate. Now that he was duke, the only limitation imposed on him was that power be exercised by the Council of Forty-Eight.

Notwithstanding his soft start, Cosimo I quickly got rid of his enemies: he defeated the faction led by Filippo Strozzi, who was found dead in prison, and succeeded in decisively eliminating all those who tried to form new pockets of resistance. In foreign policy, he abolished the old freedoms of the cities under Florentine control and subjugated them all, including Florence, to his sole power via governors whom he appointed. He created a regional state, and although the city on the Arno was its capital, the history of Florence lost its uniqueness to fit into a more clearly regional dimension. Cosimo established a strong and stable army, and in each city and along the borders he built impressive fortifications similar to the Fortezza da Basso in the northern part of Florence, built by his predecessor, Alessandro as a powerful symbol of the new authoritarian government of the city. He extended his dominions to the borders of Tuscany with a quick war, conquering Siena. Which capitulated due to hunger in 1555.

Cosimo wanted a royal crown, the recognition that would permit him to confirm his power over the territorial state. However, the rise of a descendant of a merchant family was not looked upon with favor by the main European dignitaries including the emperor, the king of France, the king of Spain and not last, the Italian princes. Nevertheless, his ties to the Church worked in his favor because Pope Pius V was a loyal friend and on 27 August 1569 conferred the title of Grand Duke of Tuscany upon Cosimo. In 1559, the Church had issued the Index of Forbidden Books (*Index Librorum Prohibitorum*), which, together with the Inquisition, had the duty of maintaining and defending the integrity of the faith, examining and prosecuting errors and false doctrines. Cosimo did not hesitate in choosing the pope as his ally.

To emphasize his new power in the city, Cosimo moved his family and court to the Palazzo della Signoria. As a result of changes made by the architect, artist and art historian, Giorgio Vasari (1511-1574) the ancient symbol of the republic became the virtual and physical symbol of the end of the republic. Still working for Cosimo, Vasari built the Uffizi, a building close to the new headquarters of the court and designed to host the ministries of the new state. The total cost of the project came to more than 400,000 *scudi*.

The Florentine merchant bankers were still doing business throughout Europe, but industry and trade were going into a slow, but steady decline and Florentines abandoned these activities to invest their money in limited partnerships. Thanks to Cosimo, and later to his sons, the new port of Livorno was founded and developed. Florentine trade flourished again with the creation of the Holy Military Order of St. Stephen Pope and Martyr in 1561; the objective of the Order's fleet was to protect the Florentine navy in the East. The grand duke helped the Florentines who were becoming more and more interested in farming by launching great land drainage and reclamation projects in the Val di Chiana, the Tuscan Maremma district and Valdinievole. These projects marked the exact moment in which Florence, now the authentic capital of Tuscany, began to neglect the distant outside world to devote its efforts to improving Tuscany.

Intellectual and artistic life continued to flourish in Florence during the reign of Cosimo I de' Medici, and architectural and artistic commissions increased. Work on the construction of the Ponte Santa Trinita continued uninterruptedly from February 1567 to January 1569. Architects such as Giuliano da Sangallo (1445-1516) and Bartolomeo Ammannati (1511-1592), sculptors and goldsmiths like Benvenuto Cellini (1500-1571), painters such as Pontormo (1494-1557) and Agnolo Bronzino (1503-1572), were commissioned to depict the symbols of the new regime.

In 1559, Eleonora de Toledo, Cosimo's very wealthy wife – daughter of the viceroy of Naples - used the money from her dowry to purchase Luca Pitti's unfinished palazzo on the other side of the Arno as the court's summer residence. In 1565, to connect the court's headquarters in Palazzo Vecchio to the new palace, Vasari brilliantly built a raised corridor running above the Ponte Vecchio through private houses and towers, allowing the duke to get around the city safely, physically and symbolically above the ordinary citizens. Having resigned from power in 1564, two years after the death of his beloved wife, Cosimo left Palazzo Vecchio to make Palazzo Pitti his permanent home and enjoy the Boboli Gardens behind it. In 1575, his son Ferdinando permanently moved the court across the Arno to Palazzo Pitti showing that the family, now firmly in power, no longer needed to reside in the center of the city.

For the first time in the history of Florence, Cosimo I de' Medici launched a campaign of political propaganda tool aimed at legitimizing the sovereign's power. Commissions proliferated, starting with the group of statues in Piazza della Signoria, rechristened Piazza del Granduca, for the purpose of exalting Cosimo's virtues and the legitimacy of his regime: *Hercules and Cacus* by Baccio Bandinelli (1534); the *Neptune Fountain* by Bartolomeo Ammannati (1575); Giambologna's *Equestrian Statue of Cosimo I* (1595); the marble group by Vincenzo Danti (1563-72) on the façade of the Uffizi, with Cosimo I as the Emperor Augustus flanked by political allegories, and the *Rape of the Sabines* by Giambologna (1579-1583). Between 1545 and 1554 Cellini cast the statue of *Perseus* for Cosimo: the Greek hero holds the head of Medusa who, even after death, still had the power to transform her enemies into stone. By placing the statue in the old loggia, with Medusa facing the city, Cosimo created a powerful symbol that 'petrified' public debate and dissent in the piazza. The two monumental columns raised in Piazza Santa Trinita (1569) and in Piazza San Felice (1570), commemorating the grand duchy's victories at Montemurlo and Marciano over the exiled Florentines who wanted to restore the republic, were similarly important from the ideological standpoint.

Even though Michelangelo died in Rome in 1564, during the thirty years that he was absent from a Florence that was no longer a republic, a productive cultural environment continued to develop in the city. Based on the model of the Platonic Academy founded by the early Medici, Giorgio Vasari established the Accademia del Disegno in 1563, and the Accademia Fiorentina, for literature and philosophy, was created in 1541 and was first headed by Benedetto Varchi. Florence had always played a leading role in the development of the Italian language: in the early fourteenth century, Dante and Boccaccio had *de facto* created the language and the Florentine merchants spread it throughout the peninsula. In the mid-fifteenth century Piero the Gouty sponsored a contest for poetry in the vernacular, despite protests from the Roman humanists for whom Latin alone was the noble language; again in Florence, Lorenzo the Magnificent had commissioned the first Tuscan grammar book. In 1583 the Accademia della Crusca was established in Florence with the purpose of regulating and disseminating the Italian language; the academy's main work, the *Vocabolario* was first published in 1612, and then expanded and republished several times until 1923.

With Cosimo's passing in 1574, the cultural fervor he had sponsored also faded. It was no longer supported by policy; the banking businesses that had brought wealth to the city went into crisis and Florence suffered a structural weakness brought about by the size of the state. The Grand Duchy of Tuscany had no more than one million inhabitants, a very small population when compared to the great nation states of modern Europe such as France and England.

Florence had to face the situation of a dynasty – that of the Medici – with no more enlightened princes. The case of Galileo Galilei (1564-1642) is emblematic of a stagnant situation. After having had Galileo tutor his children, the Grand Duke Ferdinando II (1621-1670) abandoned the mathematician from Pisa. Galilei, who supported Copernicus's heliocentric theory of the motion of heavenly bodies opposing the geocentric theory maintained by the Church, was tried by the Inquisition on 12 April 1633. Condemned for heresy on 22 June 1633, he was forced to recant his astronomical theories and sentenced to house arrest in the isolated villa he owned at Arcetri.

The exhausted dynasty dragged its weaknesses through the entire seventeenth century: under Cosimo III (1670-1722), the Medici state suffered the wretched conditions brought about by the grand duke's bad government. He was a religious fanatic who reduced

Tuscany to a 'monastic' state ruled by moralizing laws, controlled by a network of ecclesiastic spies who had to monitor the subjects' conduct, and tormented by the large sums that the grand duke paid to the clergy and to those who converted to the Roman Catholic Church. Furthermore, to maintain the luxury of the court and the costs of religious processions and services, Cosimo III imposed a tax system that struck the middle classes and destroyed the Tuscan economy.

Cosimo III's son, Giovanni Battista Gastone de' Medici, better known as Gian Gastone (1671-1737), was the last of the Medici grand dukes. He did not play any prominent role in Tuscan policies until the failure of his older brother, Ferdinando's marriage, when he was pushed to wed Princess Anna Maria Franziska of Saxe-Lauenberg in 1697. Gian Gastone ascended the throne of Tuscany in 1723. During his fourteen-year reign, and in spite of his poor health, he tried to establish a separation between Church and State, and revitalize culture by lowering taxes. Gian Gastone was a gentle, educated and peace-loving man who was openly homosexual and unhappy with his wife whose personality was the exact opposite of his. Alcohol and dissolute behavior were his solutions to sadness. The last grand duke died in 1737 without heirs. Incapable of keeping his throne independent, Gian Gastone bequeathed Tuscany to the Habsburg-Lorraine dynasty. Gian Gastone's sister, Anna Maria Luisa, was married to the Elector Palatine; she returned to Florence after her husband's death to make sure that the works of art in the Medici collections would remain in the city and never be removed. In 1737, exploiting the most modern legal instruments, she drafted the Family Pact which, in article 3, established the transfer of Medici property to the Lorraines with the proviso that the assets remain at the disposal of the city, its citizens and visitors: 'The Most Serene Electress hereby cedes, gives and transfers to H.R.H. and his successor grand dukes, all the furnishings, belongings and rarities inherited from the Most Serene Grand Duke her brother such as galleries, paintings statues, libraries, jewels and other precious things as well as the saints' Holy Relics and Reliquaries, and their ornaments of the Chapel in the Royal Palace, which H.R.H. undertakes to preserve under the express condition, that it be maintained as ornamentation of the State, for public use and to attract the curiosity of foreigners, never to be removed or transported outside of the capital and the

Grand Ducal State.' Most of the Medici's works of art were moved to the Uffizi, the former offices of the grand duchy, which Peter Leopold of Lorraine opened to the public in 1769 as one of the first museums in Europe.

13.

THE LORRAINE DYNASTY (1737-1865)

Although the end of the Medici dynasty in 1737, and the ascent to the throne of Francis Stephen, duke of Lorraine and husband of Maria Theresa of Austria, made Tuscany part of the satellite lands of the Austrian crown, the region did remain separate. After the urgent measures taken by Francis Stephen to remedy the drastic financial and economic situation caused by the ineptitude of the last Medici, the Grand Duke Peter Leopold brought Florence and Tuscany back to life by resolutely applying the principles of enlightened despotism with major reforms. The Lorraine grand ducal dynasty ruled the city calmly and was distinguished by its liberality.

While Livorno became one of the most active free ports in the Mediterranean area, where anyone could settle without fear of religious or legal persecution, on 30 November 1786, the grand duchy issued the new criminal code which, for the first time in the history of modern states, abolished the death penalty and torture. Tuscany was the first state in the world to embrace the principles of the Milanese Enlightenment philosopher Cesare Beccaria (1738-1794), who in his 1764 treatise *On Crimes and Punishments* (*Dei delitti e delle pene*) called for the abolition of capital punishment. Beccaria defined crime in lay terms, as a breach of contract: it was a matter of personal conscience and not of the public sphere. Therefore, according to Beccaria, the death penalty does not have a deterrent or intimidating effect since the criminal is less afraid of death than a life sentence or wretched slavery.

Under Peter Leopold the old organization of the guilds, the driving force behind Florentine expansion throughout the world, was suppressed. In 1770, the grand duke established a new Chamber of Commerce of Crafts and Manufactories (*Camera di Commercio delle Arti e delle Manifatture*), the first of its kind in Italy. While industry and trade were marking time, farming became the main activity in Tuscany. The

Accademia dei Georgofili was founded in Florence in 1753 by Ubaldo Montelatici, a Canon Regular of the Lateran, to promote rational and scientific farming to 'conduct continuous and well-regulated experiments and observations to perfect the so useful art of Tuscan cultivation' (*fare continue e ben regolate sperienze, ed osservazioni, per condurre a perfezione l'Arte tanto giovevole della Toscana coltivazione*).

Pursuing this course, Peter Leopold passed the agricultural reform, granting public land assets, that is communal property, grand ducal farms and secularized Church lands under perpetual leases with the possibility of redemption. By granting the grand ducal estates to peasants, or as we would call them today farmers, the grand duke hoped to start a system that would improve the agricultural workers' living conditions and release them from the servility of sharecropping.

After Peter Leopold, from 1790 to 1801 and from 1814 to 1824, came Ferdinand III of Habsburg-Lorraine (full name: *Ferdinand Josef Johann Baptist*) (1769-1824). Acting in a manner that was the exact opposite of his predecessor's, in 1814 the new Grand Duke of Tuscany abolished all communal freedoms and appointed the city's gonfaloniers himself.

Between 1801 and 1814 Florence, too, was thrown into confusion by Napoleon: the French occupation spread the ferment of national independence and liberty to the new ruling classes which the grand dukes, who were tied to Austrian policy, naturally opposed. Consequently, despite their efforts at good government and attempts at wise reforms, public opinion gradually turned against the Lorraine sovereigns.

The Grand Duke Leopold II governed Tuscany from 1824 and made every effort to turn it into a modern state by reclaiming the Maremma, in southern Tuscany, reorganizing the legal system (establishing the Civil and Criminal Courts and the Court of Cassation), building the railroad lines from Florence to Pisa and Livorno, and from Florence to Pistoia and, in 1846, establishing the first telegraph line in Italy between Florence and Pisa. Even though he also conquered the Duchy of Lucca in 1847, which had remained independent over the centuries, an abyss opened between him and his people which, given his Austrian ancestry, proved impossible to bridge. During the 1848 uprising, Leopold II fled to Rome and then to Gaeta and only returned to Florence in April 1849, supported by the Austrian troops that had defeated the King of Sardinia.

By then public opinion was simply waiting for the time to be ripe to throw out the Austrian princes and declare Italian independence. In 1859 war broke out between Austria and the King of Sardinia, backed by France. Leopold II, whose troops no longer obeyed him, abandoned Florence on 27 April 1859, never to return. In the meantime, a provisional government was established in Florence. The supporters of Tuscan independence soon turned the leadership over to those who, led by baron Bettino Ricasoli, wanted and then, through the plebiscite of 1860, achieved the annexation of the entire country, first to the Kingdom of Sardinia and then to the new Kingdom of Italy.

When the Kingdom of Italy was officially recognized on 17 March 1861, Vittorio Emanuele II, who was King of Sardinia, assumed the title of King of Italy for himself and his descendants. From the institutional and juridical standpoint, it was a kingdom that adopted the organization, rule and standards of the Kingdom of Sardinia and was therefore, *de jure*, a constitutional monarchy according to the Albertine Statute of 1848 (*Statuto Albertino*). Therefore, it was the king who appointed the government which was, in turn, answerable to the sovereign and not the parliament; it was up to the king to maintain prerogatives in foreign policy and to choose the government ministers in the customary manner.

However, the Italian peninsula was not completely unified until the Republic of Venice joined the Kingdom of Italy in 1866, and it was only in 1870 that the kingdom's troops entered Rome. Florence, with its excellent geographic location and important history, immediately became one of the new nation's important cities. In 1861 it hosted the first Italian exposition showcasing the industry and crafts of all the Italian regions. Perceived as the cradle and center of the Italian language, Massimo d'Azeglio (1798-1866) said that Florence should be the capital of Italy while awaiting the conquest of Rome which, as we have seen, only occurred ten years later. And so, Florence was chosen to be the capital of the new Kingdom of Italy in 1865.

14.

FLORENCE, CAPITAL OF THE KINGDOM OF ITALY (1865-1871)

Florence was the capital of Italy for six years, from 3 February 1865 to 30 June 1871. During that short period the city's history was reinterpreted and analyzed in preparation for the attempt to replace the culture that the Renaissance territorial states had developed over time – I refer to Venice, Milan, Turin, Florence, Rome, Naples – with the shared identity of a united Italy. The installation of the royal court and the ministers of the Kingdom of Italy in the most important city of central Italy set Florentine life topsy-turvy, augmenting the growth of traditional activities and enriching it with new ones. In 1851 Florence had a population of approximately 110,000; when it became the capital there was an influx of around 30,000 people, mainly from Piedmont. The majority of the newcomers comprised the staff of the newly-established Kingdom of Italy. It was relatively easy to locate the new offices and public services in the buildings of an old capital abounding in the splendid and immense palaces of Late-Medieval merchants. The royal court took over Palazzo Pitti, the former Medici and then Lorraine residence; the parliament and the ministry for foreign affairs were installed in Palazzo della Signoria, the seat of the republican commune until the end of the sixteenth century; the ministry of the interior was set up in Palazzo Medici, the first home of the family of bankers.

Housing, however, created serious problems for the city where, up to then, the area within the circle of walls begun in 1284 and completed in 1333 was just about sufficient. The historical center was gutted in an 'Improvement Program' (*Risanamento*) that led to the demolition of the old medieval blocks and the construction of new neighborhoods in the area of Piazza d'Azeglio and then Campo di Marte. Through these programs, the price of housing increased tenfold and the less prosperous classes found themselves forced to move away from the city center. After centuries of demographic stability, the number of citizens of Florence rose from approximately 146,000 to over 200,000, an increase of more than one third. More than 50,000 apartments were built between 1865 and 1871; 1,800 of them were located in the area near Piazza d'Azeglio. The problem was that they were not enough.

Giuseppe Poggi, a very talented architect, created an expansion plan that called for tearing down the Dante-era walls on the right bank of the Arno and replacing them with wide, tree-shaded boulevards, interrupted by symmetrical plazas built in the areas of the ancient city gates. Poggi then created a magnificent tree-lined avenue, the Viale de' Colli, that leads to Piazzale Michelangelo, the spectacular belvedere overlooking the city. In the center, he enlarged the main streets and built a large square in the area that was once the Roman forum and later the medieval marketplace. This radical reorganization of the city that led, not without much argument, to the demolition of large portions of the historic center that were considered unhealthy and unlivable, included the completion of old monuments. The nineteenth century brought Florence the opportunity to finally complete two of the city's major churches: the Franciscan basilica of Santa Croce and the cathedral of Santa Maria del Fiore. Construction of both had started at the end of the thirteenth century, and the façades had remained rough and non-decorated due to a lack of funds. Between 1853 and 1863 the architect Niccolò Matas designed the façade of Santa Croce, taking his inspiration for the evenly alternating colored marbles and the pinnacles from the façades of Tuscan Gothic churches, such as Siena and Orvieto. The local success of this project prompted the Florentines to announce a competition for the completion of the cathedral. Here too, the choice fell on colored marble, identical to the fourteenth-century decorations on the sides of the church and the bell tower, with a myriad of statues of prophets and apostles set into elaborate niches.

The intellectual and artistic movement that for twenty years had made Florence the spiritual center of the new Italy, gained strength from the presence of the government bodies. In his capacity as senator of the Kingdom of Italy, the writer Alessandro Manzoni recommended that the principals of the elementary schools of the new Kingdom of Italy hire Tuscan teachers, urging them to offer their students study trips to the city on the banks of the Arno, convinced that the language of Dante could educate the young generations and therefore complete the difficult road towards unity. The publisher Le Monnier (1833), the newspaper *La Nazione* (1859), the journals *Nuova Antologia* and *Archivio Storico Italiano* contributed to the creation of the new country's linguistic and cultural unity. The Liceo Dante (founded in 1863) and the Istituto di Studi Superiori Pratici e di Perfezionamento (1858-1924) became teaching laboratories for training and educating the new Italian ruling class. During those years certain, only apparently minor, figures were central to the city's intellectual life.

There was the archivist, Cesare Guasti whose meticulous work reorganized the Archivio di Stato of Florence and helped new generations of scholars (myself included) to start studying Medieval primary sources in a uniform key. The twenty-nine-year-old Giovanni Verga, destined to become one of Italy's most important writers, reached the banks of the Arno on 29 April 1869 from his native Sicily; in a letter to his brother Mario, dated 7 May 1869, he described Florence as 'the center of Italian political and intellectual life.'

Florence, as capital, did not overlook social issues and restored ancient charitable institutions such as the Bigallo and the Spedale degli Innocenti to renewed splendor. As a symbol of its technological and educational progress, at the 1900 *Exposition Universelle* in Paris Italy exhibited a series of photographs – taken by the Stabilimento Fotografico Brogi – documenting the history of the Spedale degli Innocenti.

The list of artisans and professionals working in Florence during that period was considerable, and it is interesting to note that the wine-sellers took first place with 374 shops. Drinking water was still hard to come by in the second half of the nineteenth century, so wine continued to be the people's main beverage.

As capital, Florence also increased the sites and venues dedicated to leisure time, building marvelous fashionable cafes, new cultural venues such as academies and libraries, as well as luxurious hotels and – strange as it may seem – even brothels to entertain visitors and tourists. Among the cultural venues it is important to mention the Biblioteca Nazionale Centrale, established by a decree dated 22 December 1861: in 1871, when Florence was still capital of the Kingdom of Italy, it was open daily from 9:00 a.m. to 4:00 p.m.– except for holidays.

Business discovered new strategies, aimed at new horizons, and acquired different administrative and technological skills. Paradigmatic examples are the Fonderia del Pignone, a factory built outside the Porta San Frediano in 1842 that used iron ore from the Island of Elba, and Ceramiche Ginori, established in 1735 in Florence, in the Grand Duchy of Tuscany, by the great thinker and entrepreneur Marquis Carlo Andrea Ginori, both restored to new life in the 1860s. Notwithstanding all these changes, growth did not bring improvements in living conditions since the less prosperous classes continued to suffer from a shortage of food.

During the second half of the nineteenth century there were many women who worked, but they had no rights. They worked in the tobacco factory, in the world of fashion, manufacturing textiles, especially wool and silk, while a considerable number made the Leghorn (straw) hats that were in great demand among the emerging classes of the new united Italy. The glorious tradition of the illustrious Renaissance Florentines made it possible for the city to become the capital of the young nation in the years that the West was struggling to find new forms of political stability.

15.

FLORENCE, CITY OF ART (1871-1967)

The entry of Italian troops into Rome on 20 September 1870 marked the end of the Papal State. The following year, according to the provisions of Law 33 of 3 February 1871, the capital of Italy was transferred from Florence to Rome. Florence was once again a large regional center and since Tuscany was essentially agricultural, the city again became a huge market for wine, oil, grain and livestock. The Chamber of Commerce, *Camera di Commercio*, was renamed Chamber of Commerce, Agriculture and Industry (*Camera di Commercio, Agricoltura e Industria*). At what was the dawn of the machine age in Europe, in Florence there were only two industrial factories in, the above-mentioned Fonderia del Pignone and the Officine Galileo, which produced precision instruments and optics.

However, notwithstanding the departure of the court and the government, Florence continued with its urbanistic and cultural transformation. The grand abandoned palaces became home to museums and cultural associations that continued to celebrate the essential values through which it could still claim to be the capital of Italy: did it not already possess the literary pantheon in Santa Croce where the funerary monuments to the Renaissance geniuses Salutati, Bruni, Michelangelo and Machiavelli, were flanked by those of the greatest writer-scholars of modern Italy, Alfieri and Foscolo?

Florence, the cradle of Humanism, was constantly visited and praised by foreign authors, such as the British writer, painter and art critic John Ruskin (1819-1900), whose *Mornings in Florence* (1875) presents an unusual tour of Santa Croce, and the French author, Anatole France (1844-1924), whose *Le lys rouge* (*The Red Lily*), published in 1894 highlights the city's intellectual and artistic calling. Florentine novelists were equally important, and they used the city as the setting for their works: Aldo Palazzeschi, author of *Sorelle Materassi* (1934), and Vasco Pratolini, author of *Il Quartiere (The Naked Streets)* (1943),

Cronaca familiare (Family Chronicle) (1947), *Le ragazze di San Frediano (The Girls of Sanfrediano)* (1952).

During the first half of the twentieth century, Florence continued as Italy's intellectual center. Cultural output consisted primarily of the emergence of magazines illustrating the new trends among Italian writers. *Lacerba* magazine (1913-1915), founded by the painter Ardengo Soffici and the critic and novelist Giovanni Papini, was the voice of a mystical current which, from its earliest days, became one of the constants in a Florence that often appeared purely intellectual and skeptical. Other important endeavors included *La Voce* (1908-1916) founded by Giuseppe Prezzolini and later edited by Giuseppe De Robertis, and *Solaria*, established in 1926 by Alberto Carocci in liaison with Eugenio Montale, Leone Ginzburg, Aldo Garosci, Guglielmo Alberti and Giacomo Debenedetti. Publication of *Solaria* ceased in 1936 during the Fascist era, but the banner of Florence would again be raised high after the Second World War through journals such as *Belfagor*, founded by Luigi Russo in 1946, which was published every two years until 30 November 2012.

When Italy entered the Second World War, the city's monuments were protected as far as possible: statues were crated and surrounded with sandbags, many chapels were walled up, the stained-glass windows of the main churches were removed and taken to safe places. The bombing of Pisa at the end of 1942 raised fears about the works of art in Florence: many were taken from the museums to the Medici villas at Cafaggiolo and Poggio a Caiano.

The situation deteriorated rapidly after the armistice of 8 September 1943. German troops entered the city three days later (11 September) and on 25 September the American 97th Bomber Group, with thirty-nine B-17s, dropped bombs on Florence to strike the Campo di Marte rail hub. But they missed the target and bombs fell on the area of the Giardino dell'Orticoltura, close to the municipal stadium and near the English Cemetery in Piazzale Donatello, killing two hundred and fifteen people and injuring countless others.

To block the Allies' advance, the Germans decided to mine the city's bridges. The Ponte alle Grazie was blown up at 10:00 p.m. on 3 August 1944; at 4:00 a.m. the next day all the other bridges, Ponte Santa Trinita, Ponte alla Carraia, Ponte alla Vittoria met the same fate. Only the Ponte Vecchio was spared, but the surrounding neighborhoods were severely damaged. What is known as the 'Battle of

Florence' ended on 11 August 1944, but with untold damage to the city's heritage.

After the the Second World War, Florence became one of Italy's most important publishing cities. The crafts continued to maintain qualities that were unique in Italy, Europe and throughout the world in products ranging from linens to embroideries, mosaics, carved wood, metals, artistic glass, plaited straw, ceramics and porcelain (the Manifattura Richard Ginori, for example), and fine leather goods (the Santa Croce Leather School - *Scuola di Cuoio*). These successes carried Florence into the realms of high fashion, Gucci, and luxury footwear, Ferragamo. The most famous and the less-renowned Florentine names displayed along Via Tornabuoni began opening stores on the most important streets in Paris, London, New York, Los Angeles, Tokyo and Hong Kong.

The unanimously acknowledged splendor of Florentine culture explains the emotional shock with which public opinion learned of the catastrophe that struck the city and surrounding countryside in the autumn of 1966. The first documented flood of the Arno occurred in 1177. Since then at more or less regular intervals the river overflowed its banks in the fall, early in November, fifty-six times. On the morning of Friday, 4 November 1966 after torrential rains, equaling between 25 and 30% of the city's annual precipitation within forty-eight hours, the Arno overflowed its banks and rushed through the city. A particularly violent wave swept through the Santa Croce district and many currents crisscrossed the slight depression where the cathedral and baptistery stand. Forty percent of the city was severely damaged. To find a comparable disaster we have to reread the words of the fourteenth-century chronicler Giovanni Villani who had described the flood of 1333 and the destruction of the Ponte Vecchio.

The water rushed through the city's streets and killed about thirty people, a figure which, unfortunately, has never been confirmed by the authorities. The furious waters invaded workshops, cellars and the ground floors of homes, churches and museums. Water, diesel fuel and oil filled the basilica of Santa Croce up to a height of six meters and many works of art were irreparably damaged because the water was mixed with fuel from boilers and automobile engines. Once the water was eliminated from the surface of the enormous, late-thirteenth-century crucifix by Cimabue, it became covered with blisters that began to burst so that more than half the paint layer flaked and disintegrated.

The flood left slimy mud filled with wrecks of all kinds, stained walls, more than a thousand damaged paintings, and over three hundred thousand illegible books in the Biblioteca Nazionale. The University of Florence lost roughly one hundred thousand books from its collections and five kilometers of shelves filled with archive documents were irreparably damaged, along with countless works of art that had been submerged for hours. Within a few weeks, tons of books were retrieved from the mud and taken to safe places where they were dried and hastily cleaned. The task of salvaging, cleaning and restoring the damaged items began and the Florentine community welcomed help from all over the world. Blotting paper was placed between the pages of manuscripts; the damaged paintings were taken to the *Orangerie* at Palazzo Pitti where cleaning and protective procedures were conducted using rice paper, cellulose pulp and acrylic resins. This marked the beginning of a long and delicate labor to prevent wood from rotting, to remove mildew from books and documents, to restore the splendor of stone and marble and also to consolidate the supports of paintings and, if necessary, replace them.

CONCLUSION
FLORENCE AND ITS LEGEND

As a result of its unique monuments and the works of its exceptionally vast array of brilliant men, even today Florence still boasts its unique originality, its position as Italy's intellectual fulcrum and its universal calling. The city's spirit, its 'virtues', are still intact in an agglomeration with more than half a million inhabitants. Its prosperity makes the city one of the finest examples of the spirit so avidly sought by the humanists. Consequently, tourism is one of the major businesses in today's Florence; it is a business based directly on the grandeur and beauty bequeathed by the geniuses – the Renaissance men and the bankers and traders. The wealthy eighteenth-century travelers, the nineteenth-century artists, scholars and aesthetes are being followed by the hordes of twentieth and early-twenty-first century tourists who come from all over the world to contemplate marvelous works of art in a setting that has remained more or less intact over the centuries.

Today, Florence is living off the work, intelligence and brilliance of the Renaissance entrepreneurs. Albeit with changes, it has maintained its universal character, which depends not so much on expanding its markets and selling its products as on the universal qualities of the masterpieces it holds and the different origins of the crowds that come to visit. The legend of Florence gained strength in the second half of the nineteenth century, and specifically when Florence became the capital of the new Kingdom of Italy. In this context, Florence began to be perceived as one of the foundations of the entire Western World. Universities gradually began offering their first courses in European history, in which the Florentine model was a crucial point; countless university departments were established overseas after the trauma of the First World War, fitting into the new category of Western Civilization, further strengthening and expanding Florence's importance as a benchmark of Western culture.

It seems that Florence is truly a paradigmatic city within the global collective vision. It continues to be the city in which the collective mind sees the long process that led to modernity, perhaps because – more than any other geopolitical entity in modern Italy – it is perceived as one of the symbolic places for best understanding the dynamics of Western democracy. Florence is a cultural model through which even today we can trace the beginnings of democracy, liberty, rational thought and scientific method. In 1890 a seventeen-year-old youth arrived in Florence from Molfetta in Puglia. Gaetano Salvemini (1873-1957) came to study at the school that the future minister of education, Pasquale Villari established at the Istituto di Studi Superiori. This youth, who would become one of the leading intellectuals in the Italy of the first half of the twentieth century, owed everything to the cultural climate that developed when Florence was the capital of the new Kingdom of Italy. His medievalist studies covered a relatively limited period, the communal era, or rather the 'Age of Dante'. To say that they were fundamental is an understatement because, for the first time they highlighted the risks that create crises for republican systems. His studies showed that it was the people who wanted the laws, the *Ordinamenti di giustizia* of 1293, against the magnates, and that it was the new bourgeoisie class, like the magnates of the past, that wanted to adopt an essentially anti-democratic political approach. Gaetano Salvemini was twenty-six years old in 1899 when, (under the auspices of the Istituto di Studi Superiori) he published *Magnati e popolani in Firenze dal 1280 al 1295*, an unsurpassed book that, in a Marxist key, presents the struggle between the magnates and *popolani* as one of the earliest examples of class struggle. In his acknowledgments Salvemini wrote: 'As I conclude this book, written following the teachings and examples of the professors of the Istituto di Studi Superiori in Florence, I wish to publicly express my profound gratitude to the teachers from whom I learned the method of scientific research and the passion for work. I am especially grateful to professors Villari, Paoli, and Del Vecchio who, throughout the course of this study, were always generous with their advice, encouragement and help. I am also indebted to Professor Isidoro del Lungo for his many useful suggestions and hence, to him my warmest thanks'.

To borrow Salvemini's words, it is via the path of culture and research that Florence is clearing the main road that the Western world will travel in the years to come. A medieval city of great commerce shining its light beyond the boundaries of Christendom, a privileged city of intelligence and liberty. After having made such a great contribution to the creation of a united Italy by giving it a language and being its capital, Florence, cradle of humanism and of the Renaissance men whose genius knew no bounds, seems destined to be part of the common spirit of Western Christendom that is Europe in the twenty-first century.

BIBLIOGRAPHY

General Bibliography

Bargellini, Piero, *Florence the Magnificent: a History* (Florence: Vallecchi, 1980).
Borsook, Eve, *Ecco Firenze. Guida ai luoghi nel tempo* (Milan: Mursia, 1972).
Borsook, Eve, *The Companion Guide to Florence* (London: Collins, 1985).
Brucker, Gene A. *Florence, the Golden Age, 1138-1737* (Berkley: University of California Press, 1993).
Cardini, Franco, *A Short History of Florence* (Pisa: Pacini, 1999).
Cardini, Franco, *An Illustrated History of Florence* (Pisa: Pacini, 2007).
Davidsohn, Robert, *Forschungen zur älteren Geschichte von Florenz* (Berlin: Mittler und Sohn, 1896-1908).
Davidsohn, Robert, *Geschichte von Florenz, mit einem Stadtplan* (Berlin: Ernst Siegfried Mittler und Sohn, 1896-1927) [Italian Translation: Davidsohn, Robert, *Storia di Firenze*, vols I-VIII (Florence: Sansoni 1956-68)].
Detti, Edoardo, *Florence that Was* (Florence: Vallecchi, 1970).
Fanelli, Giovanni, *Firenze* (Rome and Bari: Laterza, 1988).
Fei, Silvano Gobbi Sica, Grazia, Sica, Paolo, *Firenze: profilo di storia urbana - Florence: an Outline of Urban History* (Florence: Alinea, 1995).
Ginori Lisci, Leonardo, *I palazzi di Firenze nella storia e nell'arte* (Florence: Cassa di Risparmio, 1972).
Ginori Lisci, Leonardo, *The Palazzi of Florence* (Florence: Barbera, 1985)
Gurrieri, Francesco; Fabbri, Patrizia, *Palaces of Florence* (San Giovanni Lupatoto: Arsenale, 1995).
Hibbert, Christopher, *Florence: the Biography of a City* (London: Penguin,1994)
Listri, Pier Francesco, Naldini, Maurizio, *La costruzione della bellezza. Duemila anni di storia di Firenze* (Florence: Clichy, 2013).
Macadam, Alta, *City Guide. Florence* (London: A & C Black; New York: W.W. Norton, 2001).
Macarthy, Mary, *The Stones of Florence* (San Francisco: Normanby Press, 2016)
Martucci, Roberto; Giovannetti, Bruno, *Florence: Guide to the Principal Buildings. History of Architecture and Urban Form* (Venice: Canal & Stamperia, 1997).

Najemy, John M. *A History of Florence 1200-1575* (Oxford: Blackwell, 2006).
Paatz, Walter, *Die Kirchen von Florenz. Ein Kunstgeschichtliches Handbuch*, 6 voll. (Frankfurt a. M.: Klostermann, 1940-1954).
Spadolini, Giovanni, *Firenze. Mille anni* [1964] (Florence: Le Monnier, 1984).

Select Bibliography by Chapter

Chapter 1. The Roman City (59 a.C. - 1138)

Archeologia a Firenze: città e territorio, ed. by Valeria d'Aquino (Oxford: Archaeopress, 2015).
Atlante archeologico di Firenze: indagine storico-archeologica dalla preistoria all'Alto Medioevo, ed. by Mario Pagni (Florence: Polistampa, 2010).
Capecchi, Gabriella, *Alle Origini di Firenze: dalla preistoria alla città romana* (Florence: Polistampa, 1996).
Chiostri, Frido, *L'acquedotto romano di Firenze* (Florence: Centro Editoriale Toscano, 2002).
Degl'Innocenti, Piero, *Le origini del bel San Giovanni: da tempio di Marte a Battistero di Firenze* (Florence: Libreria Alfani, 2014).
Hardie, Colin, 'The Origin and Plain of Roman Florence', *The Journal of Roman Studies*, 55,1/2 (1965), pp. 122-140.
Lunga memoria della piana. L'area fiorentina dalla preistoria alla romanizzazione, ed. by Fabio Martini, Gabriella Poggesi, Lucia Sarti (Pontassieve: Centro Stampa, 1999).
Maetzke Guglielmo, *Florentia (Firenze). Regio VII - Etruria, Italia romana: Municipi e Colonie*, I, 5, (Rome: Istituto di Studi Romani, 1941).
Maetzke, Guglielmo, 'Gli scavi di Piazza della Signoria a Firenze', *Prospettiva*, 3 (1975), pp. 64-66.
Mensi, Elisa, *La Fortezza di Firenze e il suo territorio in epoca romana* (Florence: Olschki, 1991).
Salvestrini, Francesco, *Libera città su fiume regale. Firenze e l'Arno dall'Antichità al Quattrocento* (Florence: Nardini, 2005).
Scampoli, Emiliano, *Firenze, archeologia di una città: secoli I a.C.- XIII d.C.* (Florence: Firenze University Press, 2010).

Chapter 2. The City-State (1138-1216)

Benvenuti Papi, Anna, 'Un vescovo, una città: Ardingo nella Firenze del primo Duecento', in Anna Benvenuti Papi, *Pastori di popolo. Storia e leggende di vescovi e di città nell'Italia medievale* (Florence: Arnaud, 1988), pp. 21-124.
Conti, Elio, *La formazione della struttura agraria moderna nel contado fiorentino* (Rome: Istituto Storico Italiano per il Medioevo, 2014).

Cortese, Maria Elena, *Signori, castelli, città. L'aristocrazia del territorio fiorentino fra X e XII secolo* (Florence: Olschki, 2007).

Dameron, George W., *Episcopal Power and Florentine Society: 1000-1300* (Cambridge, MA, Harvard University Press, 1991).

Faini, Enrico 'I vescovi dimenticati. Memoria e oblio dei vescovi fiorentini e fiesolani dell'età pre-gregoriana', *Annali di Storia di Firenze*, VIII (2013), pp. 11-49.

Faini, Enrico, *Firenze nell'età romanica (1000-1211). L'espansione urbana, lo sviluppo istituzionale, il rapporto con il territorio* (Florence: Olschki, 2010).

Firenze prima degli Uffizi. Lo scavo di via de' Castellani: contributi per un'archeologia urbana fra tardo antico ed età moderna, ed. by Riccardo Francovich, Federico Cantini, Carlotta Cianferoni, Emiliano Scampoli (Florence: All'insegna del Giglio, 2007).

Firenze prima di Arnolfo: retroterra di grandezza, ed. by Timothy Verdon (Florence: Mandragora, 2016).

Giusti, Anna Maria, *The Baptistery of San Giovanni* (Florence: Mandragora, 2000)

Le radici cristiane di Firenze, ed. by Anna Benvenuti, Franco Cardini, Elena Giannarelli (Florence: Alinea, 1994).

Pirillo, Paolo, *Firenze. Il vescovo e la città nell'Alto Medioevo*, in *Vescovo e città nell'Alto Medioevo: quadri generali e realtà toscane*, ed. by Giampaolo Francesconi (Pistoia: Centro Italiano di Studi di Storia e d'Arte, 2001), pp. 181-201.

Salvestrini, Francesco, 'La prova del fuoco. Vita religiosa e identità cittadina nella tradizione del monachesimo fiorentino (seconda metà del secolo XI)', *Studi Medievali*, LVII, I (2016), pp. 87-128.

Vannini, Guido, 'Florentia altomedievale: le mura carolinge, storia e topografia di un mito di fondazione', in *Metodologia, insediamenti urbani e produzioni. Il contributo di Gabriella Maetzke e le attuali prospettive delle ricerche* (Viterbo: Università degli studi della Tuscia, 2008), pp. 437-478.

Chapter 3. Guelphs and Ghibellines (1216-1237)

Bruni, Francesco, *La città divisa. Le parti e il bene comune da Dante a Guicciardini* (Bologna: Il Mulino, 2003).

Caggese, Romolo, *Roberto d'Angiò e i suoi tempi* (Florence: Bemporad, 1922).

De Rosa, Daniela, *Alle origini della Repubblica fiorentina. Dai consoli al 'primo Popolo" (1172-1260)* (Florence: Arnaud, 1995).

Francovich, Riccardo, *I castelli del contado fiorentino nei secoli XII e XIII* (Florence: Edizioni CLUSF, 1973).

Ghibellini, guelfi e popolo grasso. I detentori del potere politico a Firenze nella seconda metà del Duecento, ed. by Raveggi, Sergio, Tarassi, Mario, Medici, Daniela, Parenti, Patrizia (Florence: La Nuova Italia, 1978).

Guelfi e ghibellini nell'Italia del Rinascimento, ed. by Marco Gentile (Rome: Viella, 2005).

Maire Vigueur, Jean-Claude, 'Il problema storiografico: Firenze come modello (e mito) del regime popolare', in *Magnati e popolani nell'età comunale* (Pistoia: Centro Italiano di Studi di Storia e d'Arte, 1997), pp. 1-16.

Ricciardelli, Fabrizio, 'Confini e bandi: azione politica a Firenze in età comunale', in *Images and Words in Exile: Avignon and Italy during the First Half of the 14th Century*, ed. by Elisa Brilli, Laura Fenelli, and Gerhard Wolf (Florence: Edizioni del Galluzzo, 2015).

Ricciardelli, Fabrizio, 'The Emotional Language of Justice in Late Medieval Italy', in *Emotions, Passion, and Power in Renaissance* Italy, ed. by Fabrizio Ricciardelli and Andrea Zorzi (Amsterdam: Amsterdam University Press, 2015), pp. 31-43.

Ricciardelli, Fabrizio, *The Politics of Exclusion in Early Renaissance Florence* (Turnhout: Brepols, 2007).

Sznura, Franek, *L'espansione urbana di Firenze nel Dugento* (Florence: La Nuova Italia, 1975).

Chapter 4. The Rise of the *popolo* (1237-1293)

Diacciati, Silvia, *Popolani e magnati: società e politica nella Firenze del Duecento*, presentazione di Jean-Claude Maire Vigueur (Spoleto: Fondazione Centro Italiano di Studi sull'Alto Medioevo, 2011).

Il libro del chiodo, ed. by Fabrizio Ricciardelli (Rome: Istituto Storico Italiano per il Medioevo, 1998).

Ottokar, Nicola, *Il comune di Firenze alla fine del Dugento* (Rome: Vallecchi, 1926).

Raveggi, Sergio, 'Appunti sulle forme di propaganda nel conflitto tra magnati e popolani', in *Le forme della propaganda politica nel Due e nel Trecento* (Rome: École Française de Rome, 1994), pp. 469-489.

Raveggi, Sergio et al., *Ghibellini, guelfi e popolo grasso. I detentori del potere politico a Firenze nella seconda metà del Duecento* (Florence: La Nuova Italia, 1978).

Salvemini, Gaetano, *La dignità cavalleresca nel Comune di Firenze e altri scritti*, ed. by Ernesto Sestan (Milan: Feltrinelli, 1972).

Salvemini, Gaetano, *Magnati e popolani in Firenze dal 1280 al 1295* (Florence: Carnesecchi, 1899).

Zorzi, Andrea, 'I rettori di Firenze. Reclutamento, flussi, scambi (1193-1313)', in *I podestà dell'Italia comunale*, I, *Reclutamento e circolazione degli ufficiali forestieri (fine XII sec.-metà XIV sec.)*, ed. by Jean-Claude Maire Vigueur, vol. I (Rome: Istituto Storico Italiano per il Medioevo, 2000), pp. 453-594.

Zorzi, Andrea, *L'amministrazione della giustizia penale nella Repubblica fiorentina. Aspetti e problemi* (Florence: Olschki, 1988).

Zorzi, Andrea, 'L'organizzazione del territorio in area fiorentina tra XIII e XIV secolo', in *L'organizzazione del territorio in Italia e in Germania: secoli XIII-XIV*, ed. by Giorgio Chittolini, Dietmar Willoweit (Bologna: Il Mulino, 1994), pp. 279-349.

Zorzi, Andrea, *La trasformazione di un quadro politico. Ricerche su politica e giustizia a Firenze dal Comune allo Stato territoriale* (Florence: Firenze University Press, 2008).

Zorzi, Andrea, 'The 'Popolo': Social Transformations and Political Developments', in *Italy in the Age of the Renaissance, 1250-1530*, ed. by John M. Najemy (Oxford: Oxford University Press, 2004), pp. 145-164.

Chapter 5. The City of Arnolfo, Dante and Giotto (1282-1348)

Antonetti, Pierre, *La vita quotidiana a Firenze ai tempi di Dante* (Milan: BUR Rizzoli, 2017).

Arnolfo: alle origini del Rinascimento fiorentino, ed. by Enrica Neri Lusanna (Florence: Polistampa, 2005).

Brilli, Elisa, *Firenze e il profeta. Dante tra teologia e politica* (Rome: Carocci, 2012).

Come albero fiorito: Firenze tra Medioevo e Rinascimento ed. by Silvia Diacciati (Florence: Mandragora, 2016).

Dameron, George W., *Florence and its Church in the Age of Dante* (Philadelphia: University of Pennsylvania Press, 2005).

Duomo e battistero di Firenze, ed. by Piero Sanpaolesi and Mario Bucci (Florence: Sansoni, 1966).

Finn, David, *The Florence Baptistery Doors* (London: Thames and Hudson, 1980).

Firenze al tempo di Dante. Documenti sull'urbanistica fiorentina, ed. by Guido Pampaloni (Rome: Pubblicazioni degli Archivi di Stato, Fonti e Sussidi, 1973).

Firenze: le porte dell'ultima cerchia di mura, ed. by Renzo Manetti and Maria Chiara Pozzana (Florence: CLUSF, 1979).

Paolozzi Strozzi, Beatrice, *The Basilica of Santa Croce: Itinerary Guide* (Livorno: Sillabe, 2003).

Ricciardelli, Fabrizio, '«In nome di Dio e del guadagno». Giotto imprenditore tra francescanesimo e mondo degli affari', *Rivista di letteratura storiografica italiana*, I, 2017, pp. 9-25.

Ricciardelli, Fabrizio, *The Myth of Republicanism in Renaissance Italy* (Turnhout: Brepols, 2015).

Rubinstein, Nicolai *The Palazzo Vecchio 1298-1532: Government, Architecture, and Imagery in the Civic Palace of the Florentine Republic* (Oxford: Clarendon Press, 1995).

S. Maria del Fiore: teorie e storie dell'archeologia e del restauro nella città delle fabbriche arnolfiane, ed by Giuseppe Rocchi Coopmans de Yoldi (Florence: Alinea Editrice, 2006).

Saalman, Howard, *The Church of Santa Trinita in Florence* (New York: The College Art Association of America, 1966).

The Cambridge Companion to Dante, ed. by Rachel Jacoff (Cambridge, MA: Cambridge University Press, 1993).

Chapter 6. A City of Merchants (1282-1348)

Astorri, Antonella, *La Mercanzia a Firenze nella prima metà del Trecento. Il potere dei grandi mercanti* (Florence: Olschki, 1998).

Becker, Marvin, 'A Study in Political Failure. The Florentine Magnates: 1280-1343', *Mediaeval Studies*, 27 (1965), pp. 246-308.

Becker, Marvin, *Florence in Transition. I. The Decline of the Comune. II. Studies in the Rise of the Territorial State* (Baltimore: The Johns Hopkins Press, 1967).

Brown, Judith C. and Goodman, Jordan, 'Women and Industry in Florence', *The Journal of Economic History*, 40 (1980), pp. 73-80.

Brucker, Gene A., *Florentine Politics and Society: 1343-1378* (Princeton: Princeton University Press, 1962).

Brucker, Gene A., *The Civic World of Early Renaissance Florence* (Princeton: Princeton University Press, 1977).

Dini, Bruno, *Manifattura, commercio e banca nella Firenze medievale* (Fiesole: Nardini, 2001).

Dini, Bruno, *Saggi su un'economia-mondo. Firenze e l'Italia fra Mediterraneo ed Europa (secc. XIII-XVI)* (Pisa: Pacini, 1995).

Doren, Alfred, *Le arti fiorentine* (Florence: Le Monnier, 1940).

Franceschi, Franco, *I tedeschi e l'arte della lana a Firenze tra Tre e Quattrocento*, in *Dentro la città. Stranieri e realtà urbane nell'Europa dei secoli XII-XVI* (Pisa: GISEM; Napoli: Liguori, 1989) pp. 257-278.

Franceschi, Franco, 'Criminalità e mondo del lavoro: il tribunale dell'Arte della lana a Firenze nei secoli XIV e XV', *Ricerche storiche*, 18 (1988), pp. 551-590.

Franceschi, Franco, 'Intervento del potere centrale e ruolo delle Arti nel governo dell'economia fiorentina del Trecento e del primo Quattrocento. Linee generali', *Archivio Storico Italiano*, 151, 4 (1993), pp. 863-909.

Friedman, David, *Florentine New Towns: Urban Design in the Late Middle Ages* (New York: Architectural History Foundation, 1988).

Gualtieri, Piero, *Il Comune di Firenze tra Due e Trecento: partecipazione politica e assetto istituzionale* (Florence: Olschki, 2009).

Guidi, Guidubaldo, *I sistemi elettorali agli uffici del comune di Firenze nel primo Trecento* (Florence: Olschki, 1973).

La Roncière, Charles M., *Firenze e le sue campagne nel Trecento: mercanti, produzione, traffici* (Florence: Olschki, 2005).

Lansing, Carol, *The Florentine Magnates: Lineage and Faction in a Medieval Commune* (Princeton: Princeton University Press, 1991).

Mazzoni, Vieri, *Accusare e proscrivere il nemico politico: legislazione anti-ghibellina e persecuzione giudiziaria a Firenze (1347-1378)* (Pisa: Pacini, 2010).

Najemy, John M., *Corporatism and Consensus in Florentine Electoral Politics, 1280-1400* (Chapel Hill: The University of North Carolina Press, 1982).

Najemy, John M., 'Guild Republicanism in Trecento Florence: the Successes and Ultimate Failure of Corporate Politics', *The American Historical Review*, 84 (1979), 1, pp. 53-71.

Peterson, David S., 'The War of the Eight Saints in Florentine Memory and Oblivion', in *Society and Individual in Renaissance Florence*, ed. by William J. Connell (Berkeley: University of California Press, 2002).

Pirillo, Paolo, *Creare comunità: Firenze e i centri di nuova fondazione della Toscana medievale* (Rome: Viella, 2007).

Prato, Giuseppe, *La crisi delle compagnie mercantili dei Bardi e dei Peruzzi* (Florence: Olschki, 1926).

Sapori, Armando, *Le compagnie dei Bardi e dei Peruzzi in Inghilterra nei secoli 13. e 14.* (Florence: R. Deputazione Toscana di Storia Patria, 1923).

Tognetti, Sergio, 'Nuovi documenti sul fallimento della compagnia Frescobaldi in Inghilterra', in *Città e campagne del Basso Medioevo. Studi sulla società italiana offerti dagli allievi a Giuliano Pinto* (Florence: Olschki, 2014), pp. 135-158.

Tognetti, Sergio, *Un'industria di lusso al servizio del grande commercio: il mercato dei drappi serici e della seta nella Firenze del Quattrocento* (Florence: Olschki, 2002).

Chapter 7. The Black Plague (1348)

Cohn, Samuel K. Jr., 'The Black Death: End of a Paradigm', *The American Historical Review*, 107, 3 (2002), pp. 703-738.

Cohn, Samuel K. Jr., *The Black Death Transformed: Disease and Culture in Early Renaissance Europe* (London: Arnold, 2002).

Falsini, Aliberto Benigno, 'Firenze dopo il 1348. Le conseguenze della peste nera', *Archivio Storico Italiano*, Vol. 129, No. 4 (472) (1971), pp. 425-503.

Henderson, John, 'The Black Death in Florence: Medical and Communal Responses', in *Death in Towns: Urban Responses to the Dying and the Dead, 100-1600*, ed. by Steven Bassett (New York: Leicester University Press, 1992), pp. 136-150.

Henderson, John, *Piety and Charity in Late Medieval Florence* (Chicago-London: The University of Chicago Press, 1997).

Herlihy, David. *The Black Death and the Transformation of the West*, ed. by Samuel K. Cohn Jr. (Cambridge, MA: Harvard University Press, 1997).

Meiss, Milliard, *Painting in Florence and Siena after the Black Death: the Arts, Religion, and Society in the Mid-Fourteenth Century* (Princeton: Princeton University Press, 1978).

Chapter 8. The Tumult of the Ciompi (1378)

Becker, Marvin and Brucker, Gene A., 'The «arti minori» in Florentine Politics, 1342-1378', *Medieval studies*, 18 (1956), pp. 93-104.

Brucker, Gene A., 'The Florentine Popolo Minuto and its Political Role, 1340-1450', in *Violence and Civil Disorder in Italian Cities, 1200-1500*, ed. by Lauro Martines (Berkeley: University of California Press, 1972), pp. 155-183.

La Roncière, Charles M., *Prix et salaires à Florence au 14. siècle: 1280-1380* (Rome: École française de Rome, 1982).

De Roover, Raymond, *Labour Conditions in Florence around 1400: Theory, Policy and Reality* (London: Faber and Faber, 1968).

Franceschi, Franco, *Oltre il «Tumulto». I lavoratori fiorentini dell'arte della lana fra Tre e Quattrocento* (Florence: Olschki, 1993).

Il tumulto dei Ciompi. Un momento di storia fiorentina ed europea (Florence: Olschki, 1981).

Lantschner, Patrick, 'The 'Ciompi Revolution' Constructed: Modern Historians and the Nineteenth-Century Paradigm if Revolution', *Annali di Storia di Firenze*, IV (2009), pp. 277-297.

Stella, Alessandro, 'Les Ciompi et leurs familles', *Médiévales*, 9 (1990), 19, pp. 65-70.

Stella, Alessandro, "La bottega e i lavoranti': approche des conditions de travail des Ciompi', *Annales. Économies, sociétés, civilisations*, 44 (1989), 3, pp. 529-551.

Stella, Alessandro, *La révolte des Ciompi. Les hommes, les lieux, le travail* (Paris: École des hautes études en sciences sociales, 1993).

Trexler, Richard C., 'Il parlamento fiorentino del 1° settembre 1378', *Archivio Storico Italiano*, 143, No. 3 (525) (1985), pp. 437-475.

Chapter 9. The Oligarchic Government (1378-1434)

Brucker, Gene, *Renaissance Florence* (Berkeley: University of California Press, 1983).

Burke, Jill, *Changing Patrons: Social Identity and the Visual Arts in Renaissance Florence* (University Park: The Pennsylvania State University Press, 2004).

Burke, Peter, *Culture and Society in Renaissance Italy, 1420-1540* (London: Batsford, 1972).

Cohn, Samuel K., *The Laboring Classes in Renaissance Florence*, (New York: Academic Press, 1980).

Cohn, Samuel K., *Women in the Streets: Essays on Sex and Power in Renaissance Italy* (Baltimore and London: Johns Hopkins University Press, 1996).

Conti, Elio, *L'imposta diretta a Firenze nel Quattrocento: 1427-1494* (Rome: Istituto Storico Italiano per il Medioevo, 1984).

De Angelis, Laura, *La Repubblica di Firenze fra XIV e XV secolo: istituzioni e lotte politiche nel nascente Stato territoriale fiorentino* (Florence: Nardini, 2009).

Eckstein, Nicholas A., *The District of the Green Dragon: Neighborhood Life and Social Change in Renaissance Florence* (Florence: Olschki, 1995).

Gavitt, Philip, *Charity and Children in Renaissance Florence. The Ospedale degli Innocenti, 1410-1536* (Ann Arbor: The University of Michigan Press, 1990).

Goldthwaite, Richard A., *Banks, Palaces and Entrepreneurs in Renaissance Florence* (Aldershot, Brookfield: Variorum, 1995).

Goldthwaite, Richard A., *The Building of Renaissance Florence: an Economic and Social History* (Baltimore: The Johns Hopkins University Press, 1980)

Goldthwaite, Richard A., *The Economy of Renaissance Florence* (Baltimore: The Johns Hopkins University Press, 2009).

Guidi, Guidubaldo, *Il governo della città-repubblica di Firenze del primo Quattrocento* (Florence: Olschki, 1981).

Haines, Margaret, 'Myth and Management in the Construction of Brunelleschi's Cupola', *I Tatti Studies in the Italian Renaissance*, Vol. 14/15 (2011-2012), pp. 47-101.

Henderson, John, *Piety and Charity in Late Medieval Florence* (Chicago & London: The University of Chicago Press, 1997).

Jardine, Lisa, *Worldly Goods: a New History of the Renaissance* (New York-London: W.W. Norton, 1998).

Kent, Dale V. - Kent, Francis W., *Neighbours and Neighbourhood in Renaissance Florence: the District of the Red Lion in the Fifteenth Century* (Locust Valley, New York: J.J. Augustin, 1982).

Klapisch-Zuber, Christiane, *Ritorno alla politica: i magnati fiorentini 1340-1440* (Rome: Viella, 2009).

La città del Brunelleschi (Milan: Electa, 1991).

Lo stato territoriale fiorentino, secoli XIV-XV: ricerche, linguaggi, confronti, ed. by Andrea Zorzi; William J. Connell (Pisa: Pacini, 2001).

Martines, Lauro, *The Social World of Florentine Humanists: 1390-1460* (Toronto: University of Toronto Press, 2011).

McLean, Paul D., *The Art of the Network: Strategic Interaction and Patronage in Renaissance Florence* (Durham-London: Duke University Press, 2007).

Molho, Anthony, *Florentine Public Finances in the Early Renaissance, 1400-1433* (Cambridge, MA: Harvard University Press, 1971).

Renaissance Florence: a Social History ed. by Roger J. Crum and John T. Paoletti (Cambridge, MA: Cambridge University Press, 2006).

Ricciardelli, Fabrizio, 'La repressione del dissenso a Firenze nell'età di Cosimo de' Medici', in *Lignaggi, fazioni e conflitti nelle città spagnole e italiane del tardo Medioevo, Hispania*, Vol. 75, No 250 (2015), pp. 389-412.

Romby, Giuseppina Carla, *Descrizioni e rappresentazioni della città di Firenze nel XV secolo* (Florence: Libreria Editrice Fiorentina, 1976).

Rubinstein, Nicolai, *Florentine Studies: Politics and Society in Renaissance Florence*, ed. by Nicolai Rubinstein (Evanston: Northwestern University Press, 1968).

Society and individual in Renaissance Florence, ed. by William J. Connell (Berkeley: University of California Press, 2002).

Taddei, Ilaria, 'Il leone, la corona e lo stendardo. L'investitura della Signoria fiorentina (secoli XIV-XV)', in *I gesti del potere*, ed. by Marcello Fantoni (Florence: Le Cariti Editore, 2011), pp. 45-59.

Tanzini, Lorenzo, *Il governo delle leggi. Norme e pratiche delle istituzioni a Firenze dalla fine del Duecento all'inizio del Quattrocento* (Florence: Edifir, 2007).

Terpstra, Nicholas, *Abandoned Children of the Italian Renaissance: Orphan Care in Florence and Bologna* (Baltimore: The John Hopkins university Press, 2005).

Trachtenberg, Marvin, 'What Brunelleschi Saw: Monument and Site at the Palazzo Vecchio in Florence', *Journal of the Society of Architectural Historians*, 47, No. 1 (1988), pp. 14-44.

Trexler, Richard C., *Public Life in Renaissance Florence* (New York: Academic Press, 1980).

Turner, Richard A., *Renaissance Florence: The Invention of a New Art* (New York: Harry N. Abrams, 1997).

Chapter 10. The Medici (1434-1494)

Boschetto, Luca, *Società e cultura a Firenze al tempo del Concilio: Eugenio IV tra curiali mercanti e umanisti (1434-1443)* (Rome: Edizioni di Storia e Letteratura, 2012).

Brown, Alison, *The Medici in Florence: the Exercise and Language of Power* (Florence: Olschki, 1992).

Cesati, Franco, *The Medici* (Florence: Mandragora, 1999).

Clarke, Paula C., *The Soderini and the Medici: Power and Patronage in Fifteenth-Century Florence* (Oxford: Clarendon Press, 1991).

Consorterie politiche e mutamenti istituzionali in età laurenziana (Florence: Olschki, 1992).

De Roover, Raymond, *The Rise and the Decline of the Medici Bank: 1397-1494* (Cambridge, MA: Harvard University Press, 1963).

Fabbri, Lorenzo, *Alleanza matrimoniale e patriziato nella Firenze del '400: studio sulla famiglia Strozzi* (Florence: Olschki, 1991).

Fantoni, Marcello, *La corte del granduca: forma e simboli del potere mediceo tra Cinque e Seicento* (Rome: Bulzoni, 1994).

Fremantle, Richard, *God and Money: Florence and the Medici in the Renaissance* (Florence: Olschki, 2001).

Fubini, Riccardo, *Italia quattrocentesca: politica e diplomazia nell'età di Lorenzo il Magnifico* (Milan: Franco Angeli, 1994).

Fubini, Riccardo, *Politica e pensiero politico nell'Italia del Rinascimento: dallo Stato territoriale al Machiavelli* (Florence: Edifir, 2009).

Fubini, Riccardo, *Quattrocento fiorentino: politica, diplomazia, cultura* (Pisa: Pacini, 1996).

Hale, John Rigby, *Florence and the Medici* (London: Phoenix Press, 2001).

Jenkins, A. D. Fraser, 'Cosimo de' Medici's Patronage of Architecture and the Theory of Magnificence', *Journal of the Warburg and Courtauld Institutes*, 33 (1970), pp. 162-170.

Jurdjevic, Mark, *Guardians of Republicanism: the Valori Family in the Florentine Renaissance* (Oxford: Oxford University Press, 2008).

Kent, Dale V., *The Rise of the Medici: Faction in Florence, 1426-1434* (Oxford: Oxford University Press, 1978).

Kent, Dale, *Cosimo de' Medici and the Florentine Renaissance: The Patron's Oeuvre* (New Haven: Yale University Press, 2000).

Kent, F. W., *Princely Citizen: Lorenzo de' Medici and Renaissance Florence*, ed. by Carolyn James (Turnhout: Brepols, 2013).

Kent, Francis W., *Lorenzo de' Medici and the Art of Magnificence* (Baltimore: Johns Hopkins University Press, 2004).

Kent, Francis W., *Princely Citizen: Lorenzo de' Medici and Renaissance Florence* (Turnhout: Brepols, 2013).

Ames-Lewis, Frances, *The Early Medici and their Artists* (London: Birkbeck College, University of London, Department of History of Art, 1995).

Kent, Francis William, *Household and Lineage in Renaissance Florence: the Family Life of the Capponi, Ginori, and Rucellai* (Princeton: Princeton University Press, 1977).

Langdon, Gabrielle, *Medici Women: Portraits of Power, Love and Betrayal from the Court of Duke Cosimo I* (Toronto: University of Toronto Press, 2006).

Lorenzo il Magnifico e il suo mondo: convegno internazionale di studi, Firenze, 9-13 giugno 1992 ed. by Gian Carlo Garfagnini (Florence: Olschki, 1994).

Lorenzo the Magnificent: Culture and Politics ed. by Michael Mallet and Nicholas Mann (London: Warburg Institute, 1996).

Lucas-Dubreton, Jean, *Daily Life in Florence in the Time of the Medici* (London: Allen & Unwin, 1960).

Mantini, Silvia, *Lo spazio sacro della Firenze medicea: trasformazioni urbane e cerimoniali pubblici tra Quattrocento e Cinquecento* (Firenze: Loggia de' Lanzi, 1995)

Martines, Lauro, *April Blood. Florence and the Plot against the Medici* (London: Pimlico, 2004).

Marzi, Demetrio, *La cancelleria della Repubblica fiorentina* (Florence: Le Lettere, 1987).

Parks, Tim, *Medici Money: Banking, Metaphysics, and Art in Fifteenth-century Florence* (London: Profile Books, 2006).

Ricciardelli, Fabrizio, 'Social Control and Political Consensus in Quattrocento Florence', in *The Art and Language of Power in Renaissance Florence: Essays for Alison Brown*, ed. by Amy R. Bloch, Carolyn James, and Camilla Russell (Toronto: Centre for Reformation and Renaissance Studies, 2019), pp. 137-153.

Rubinstein, Nicolai, *The Government of Florence under the Medici: 1434 to 1494* (Oxford: Clarendon Press, 1968).

Strathern, Paul, *The Medici: Godfathers of the Renaissance* (London: Vintage books, 2003).

The Chapel of the Magi: Benozzo Gozzoli's Frescoes in the Palazzo Medici-Riccardi Florence, ed. by Cristina Acidini Luchinat (London: Thames and Hudson, 1994).

Tognetti, Sergio, *Da Figline a Firenze: ascesa economica e politica della famiglia Serristori, secoli XIV e XVI* (Florence: Opus libri, 2003).

Walter, Ingeborg, *Lorenzo il Magnifico e il suo tempo* (Rome: Donzelli, 2005).

Chapter 11. From the Republic to the Principality (1494-1530)

After civic Humanism: Learning and Politics in Renaissance Italy, ed. by Nicholas Scott Baker and Brian Jeffrey Maxson (Toronto: Centre for Reformation and Renaissance Studies, 2015).

Baron, Hans, *The Crisis of the Early Italian Renaissance: Civic Humanism and Republican Liberty in an Age of Classicism and Tyranny* (Princeton: Princeton University Press, 1967).

Brown, Alison, *Medicean and Savonarolan Florence. The Interplay of Politics, Humanism, and Religion* (Turnhout: Brepols, 2011).

Butters, Humfrey C., *Governors and Government in Early Sixteenth-Century Florence, 1502-1519* (Oxford: Clarendon Press, 1985).

Cordero, Franco, *Savonarola* (Turin: Bollati Boringhieri, 2009).

Denaro e bellezza, I banchieri, Botticelli e il rogo delle vanità, ed. by Ludovica Sebregondi, Tim Parks (Florence and Milan: Giunti, 2011).

Girolamo Savonarola, l'uomo e il frate, Atti del XXXV Convegno storico internazionale (Spoleto: CISAM, 1999).

Guidi, Guidobaldo, *Lotte, pensiero e istituzioni politiche nella Repubblica fiorentina dal 1494 al 1512* (Florence: Olschki, 1992).

Landon, William J., *Lorenzo di Filippo Strozzi and Niccolò Machiavelli* (Toronto: University of Toronto Press).

Machiavelli. Enciclopedia machiavelliana (Rome: Istituto della Enciclopedia Italiana, 2014).

Polizzotto, Lorenzo, *The Elect Nation. The Savonarolan Movement in Florence. 1494-1545* (Oxford: Clarendon Press, 1994).

Ridolfi, Roberto, *Prolegomeni ed aggiunte alla Vita di Girolamo Savonarola* (Florence: SISMEL Edizioni del Galluzzo, 2000).

The Pontificate of Clement VII: History, Politics, Culture, ed. by Kenneth Gouwens, Kenneth; Sheryl E. Reiss (Aldershot: Ashgate, 2005).

The World of Savonarola. Italian Elites and Perceptions of Crisis, Papers from the Conference Held at the University of Warwick, 29-31 May 1998, ed. by Stella Fletcher, Christine Shaw (Aldershot: Ashgate, 2000).

Sebregondi, Ludovica, *Iconografia di Girolamo Savonarola 1495-1998* (Florence: Edizioni del Galluzzo per la Fondazione Ezio Franceschini, 2004).

Una città e il suo profeta. Firenze di fronte al Savonarola, Atti del Convegno internazionale di Studi, ed. by Gian Carlo Garfagnini (Florence: SISMEL, 2001).

Von Albertini, Rudolf, *Firenze dalla Repubblica al Principato. Storia e coscienza politica* (Turin: Einaudi, 1982).

Weinstein, Donald, *Savonarola: The Rise and Fall of a Renaissance Prophet* (New Haven: Yale University Press, 2011).

Chapter 12. The Grand Duchy of Tuscany (1530-1737)

Acton, Harold, *The Last Medici* (London: Faber and Faber, 2009).

Arte e politica: l'Elettrice Palatina e l'ultima stagione della committenza medicea in San Lorenzo, ed. by Monica Bietti; Cristina Acidini Luchinat (Livorno: Sillabe, 2014).

Crum, Roger J., 'Cosmos, the World of Cosimo': The Iconography of the Uffizi Façade', *The Art Bulletin*, Vol. 71, No. 2 (Jun., 1989), pp. 237-253

Diaz, Furio, *Il granducato di Toscana. I Medici* (Turin: Unione Tipografico-Editrice Torinese, 1976).

Fletcher, Catherine, *The Black Prince of Florence: The Spectacular Life and Treacherous World of Alessandro de' Medici* (London: Vintage Books, 2017).

Gabrielle Langdon, *Medici Women. Portraits of Power, Love, and Betrayal in the Court of Duke Cosimo I* (Toronto: University of Toronto Press, 2006).

Gáldy, Andrea M., *Cosimo I de' Medici as Collector: Antiquities and Archaeology in Sixteenth-Century Florence* (Newcastle: Cambridge Scholars Publishing, 2009).

Goudriaan, Elisa, *Florentine Patricians and Their Networks: Structures Behind the Cultural Success and the Political Representation of the Medici Court (1600-1660)* (Leiden and Boston: Brill, 2018).

Gregory Murry, *The Medicean Succession: Monarchy and Sacral Politics in Duke Cosimo dei Medici's Florence* (Cambridge, MA: Harvard University Press, 2014).

Hale, John Righby, *Florence and the Medici* (London: Phoenix, 2004).

Hibbert, Christopher, *The Rise and Fall of the House of Medici* (London: Penguin, 1979).

Lippi, Donatella, *Illacrimate sepolture: curiosità e ricerca scientifica nella storia delle riesumazioni dei Medici* (Florence: Firenze University Press, 2006).

Litchfield, R. Burr, *Emergence of a Bureaucracy: the Florentine Patricians, 1530-1790* (Princeton, N.J: Princeton University Press).

Mari, Francesco, Polettini, Aldo, Lippi, Donatella, and Bertol, Elisabetta, 'The Mysterious Death of Francesco I de' Medici and Bianca Cappello: an Arsenic Murder?', *BMJ*, 333 (23–30 June 2006), 1299-1301.

Murry, Gregory, *The Medicean Succession: Monarchy and Sacral Politics in Duke Cosimo dei Medici's Florence* (Cambridge, MA: Harvard University Press, 2014).

Stillman Drake, *Galileo. A Very Short Introduction* (Oxford: Oxford University Press, 2001).

Strunck, Chistina, *Medici Women as Cultural Mediators, 1533-1743: le donne di casa Medici e il loro ruolo di mediatrici culturali fra le corti d'Europa* (Milan: Silvana, 2012).

The Cultural Politics of Duke Cosimo I de' Medici, ed. by Konrad Eisenbichler (London and New York: Routledge and Taylor et Francis Group, 2016).

The Cultural World of Eleonora di Toledo, Duchess of Florence and Siena, ed. by Konrad Eisenbichler (Aldershot: Ashgate, 2004).

Van Veen, Henk Th. *Cosimo I de' Medici and his Self-Representation in Florentine Art and Culture: From Lofty Ruler to Citizen Prince* (Cambridge, MA: Cambridge University Press, 2013).

Chapter 13. The Lorraine Dynasty (1737-1865)

Bellucci, Paolo, *I Lorena in Toscana. Gli uomini e le opere* (Florence: Edizioni Medicea, 2001).

Cochrane, Eric William, *Florence and the Forgotten Centuries 1527-1800: a History of Florence and the Florentines in the Age of Grand Dukes* (Chicago and London: The University of Chicago Press, 1974).

Contini, Alessandra; Gori, Orsola, *Dentro la reggia. Palazzo Pitti e Boboli nel Settecento* (Florence: Edifir, 2004).

Diaz, Furio, *Il Granducato di Toscana: i Lorena dalla Reggenza agli anni rivoluzionari* (Turin: UTET, 1997).

Palazzo Pitti. L'arte e la storia, ed. by Marco Chiarini (Florence: Nardini, 2000).

Spence, William Blundell, *Firenze: Guida alla capitale dei granduchi* (Siena: Nuova Immagine, 1986).

Vannucci, Marcello, *I Lorena, granduchi di Toscana* (Rome: Newton & Compton, 2003).

Vivere a Pitti: una reggia dai Medici ai Savoia, ed. by Sergio Bertelli and Renato Pasta (Florence: Olschki, 2003).

Chapter 14. Florence Capital of the Kingdom of Italy (1865-1871)

Carocci, Guido, *Firenze scomparsa: ricordi storico-artistici* (Rome: Multigrafica, 1985).
Cresti, Carlo, *Firenze, capitale mancata: architettura e città dal piano Poggi ad oggi* (Milan: Electa, 1995).
Detti, Edoardo; Detti, Tommaso, *Firenze scomparsa Il centro di Firenze restituito* (Florence: Vallecchi, 1977).
Fei, Silvano, *Firenze 1881-1898: la grande operazione urbanistica* (Rome: Officina, 1977).
Florence: Capital of the Kingdom of Italy, 1865-71, ed. by Monica Poettinger and Piero Roggi (London: Bloomsbury Academic, 2017).
Firenze 1865: quattro passi nella capitale, ed. by Lucia Bruni; Federico Napoli (Milan: Silvana Editoriale, 2014).
Giannetti; Stefano; Giannetti, Vincenzo, *Il Mercato Vecchio e il Ghetto di Firenze: com'era il cuore antico della Firenze scomparsa* (Florence: Angelo Pontecorboli Editore, 2018).
Poggi, Giuseppe, *Ricordi della vita e documenti d'arte* (Florence: Bemporad, 1909).
Una capitale e il suo architetto: eventi politici e sociali, urbanistici e architettonici. Firenze e l'opera di Giuseppe Poggi: mostra per il 150° anniversario della proclamazione di Firenze a capitale del Regno d'Italia, ed. by Loredana Maccabruni; Piero Marchi (Florence: Polistampa, 2015).
Ricciardelli, Fabrizio, 'Il 'mito' di Firenze: gli anni della capitale', *La Nuova Antologia. Rivista di lettere, scienze ed arti*, Vol. 619, Fasc. 2285 (2018), pp. 370-375.

Chapter 15. Florence City of Art (1871-1967)

Lamberini, Daniela, *Residenti anglo-americani e genius loci: ricostruzioni e restauri delle dimore fiorentine* (Rome: Bulzoni, 2000).
Gli anglo-americani a Firenze: idea e costruzione del Rinascimento. Atti del Convegno Georgetown University, Villa "Le Balze", Fiesole, 19-20 giugno 1997, ed. by Marcello Fantoni (Rome: Bulzoni, 2000).
Adamson, Walter, *Avant-Garde Florence. From Modernism to Fascism* (Cambridge, MA-London: Harvard University Press, 1993).
Il restauro dei monumenti dal 1944 al 1968. Mostra in Orsanmichele, Firenze, settembre-ottobre 1968 (Florence: Giunti and Barbera, 1968).
Vertova, Luisa, 'Restored Works of Art in Florence', *The Burlington Magazine*, Vol. 114, No. 832 (Jul., 1972), pp. 492-499.

Conclusion. Florence and its Legend

A Tale of Two Cities. Florence and Rome from the Grand Tour to Study Abroad, ed. by Portia Prebys and Fabrizio Ricciardelli (Ferrara: Edisai, 2017).

Art Cities, Cultural Districts and Museums: an Economic and Managerial Study of the Culture Sector in Florence, ed. by Luciana Lazzaretti (Florence: Florence University Press, 2004).

Chezzi, Federica, *Verso i nuovi Uffizi: la galleria e la cultura del museo dal dopoguerra a oggi* (Florence: Edifir, 2006).

Mignani Galli, Daniela, *Le botteghe di Firenze: storia dei mestieri artigiani dalle corporazioni ad oggi* (Florence: La Casa Usher, 1988).

Firenze, 1966-2016: la bellezza salvata, ed. by Cristina Acidini and Elena Capretti (Livorno: Sillabe, 2016).

The Contested Metropolis: Six Cities at the Beginning of the 21st Century (Basel: Birkhäuser, 2004).

Finito di stampare presso
POLISTAMPA FIRENZE srl
Giugno 2022